the world of tennis

the world of tennis by richard schickel

a ridge press book/random house/new york

The assistance of the National Lawn Tennis Hall
of Fame and Tennis Museum, at Newport, Rhode Island,
with special photographs for this book
is gratefully acknowledged.

Editor in Chief: Jerry Mason
Editorial Director: Adolph Suehsdorf
Art Director: Albert Squillace
Managing Editor: Moira Duggan
Art Associate: David Namias
Art Associate: Nancy Louie
Art Production: Doris Mullane
Picture Research: Marion Geisinger

Library of Congress Cataloging in Publication Data
Schickel, Richard
    The world of tennis
    "A Ridge Press Book"
    Includes index.
    1. Tennis — History. I. Title.
GV993.S34   796.34'2'09   75-10331
ISBN 0-394-49940-9

Printed and bound in Italy by Mondadori Editore, Verona.

For Sterling Lord, gratefully.

contents

introduction

This is an impressionistic book. It makes no pretense of
being a definitive history of tennis. Rather, in dealing with the game as
it has been played at the top international level—on which most
of the written sources concentrate—the effort has been to isolate and
discuss in some detail a handful of players commonly
regarded as archetypal figures of their eras. Moreover, in a relatively
limited space it has also been necessary to restrict the book's range
largely to the men and women whose reputations have been made in
singles rather than in doubles and, at that, to devote more attention to
males rather than females. These biases, alas, reflect those of tournament
directors, the press, even fans, and the author is not entirely comfortable
running with this pack. Such comfort as one derives from the knowledge
that history itself seems to endorse the criteria employed
in shaping a large body of material does not prevent the writer
from wishing that history were otherwise.

        The title of this book suggests a deeply felt imperative to
discuss something more than Wimbledon, Forest Hills, the Davis Cup.
The world of tennis is much more populous than the draws in those legendary
contests. It includes me and thee raised, these days, by many million
powers, and that presents a problem to the writer, for there are
few sources to which one can reliably turn for information about the game
as we know it, banging away at it recreationally. This being so, I
have used myself, my experiences, my opinions, as archetypal—representative
of all the hackers who love the game not wisely but too well.
I apologize for the egoism of the approach, but hope the results make
for agreeable and truthful, if occasionally idiosyncratic, reading.

        If there is a theme running through this book (other than the
author's infatuation with his subject), it is that the thrust
of tennis history has been a halting—and lately rushing—trend toward

democratization, that the villains in the tale are those
who fought to keep this good thing, this great game, the private preserve of
the affluent and socially prominent. My sympathies all lie with those—
from Tilden to Gonzales to the Aussies to Billie Jean King—who
have sought to open up the game, to place the direction
of international-class tennis in the hands of those who play it, to
demonstrate that its pleasures ought to be available to
everyone. Some of the specific results of this opening up—team tennis,
$250,000 challenge matches staged in gambling casinos—strike me
as absurd, but on the whole as good. The near-revolutionary breakthroughs
of recent years seem to me extraordinarily valuable. Strange
that the last vestiges of my inbred Middle Western populism should surface
more powerfully in the course of writing a book on tennis
than they have anywhere else.

       I have a few personal debts to pay at this point. The
largest is to my patient, skillful, companionable editor, Adie Suehsdorf, who
is about the best doubles partner I've ever had in the book game. He never
poaches, but he has saved more points for the team than I enjoy admitting.
Marty Bell of *Sport* magazine gave me an assignment that enabled
me to gather the material in Chapter Nine and was a knowing, patient guide to
the intricacies of a modern tennis tournament. My wife, Julia Whedon,
and my friend, Joseph Andrew Hays, provided me with extra sets of keen eyes at
Forest Hills in 1974, and the former has contributed more than she.
knows to this book with her sensible comments on the game we both love
better than we play. Finally, I must thank the hundreds of people
who have contributed to my knowledge of my subject by playing with and
against me. I don't know which of those roles requires the most
patience, but I wish them all magical increases in the cunning of their
racket hands—except, of course, in certain obvious instances.

Richard Schickel
New York City

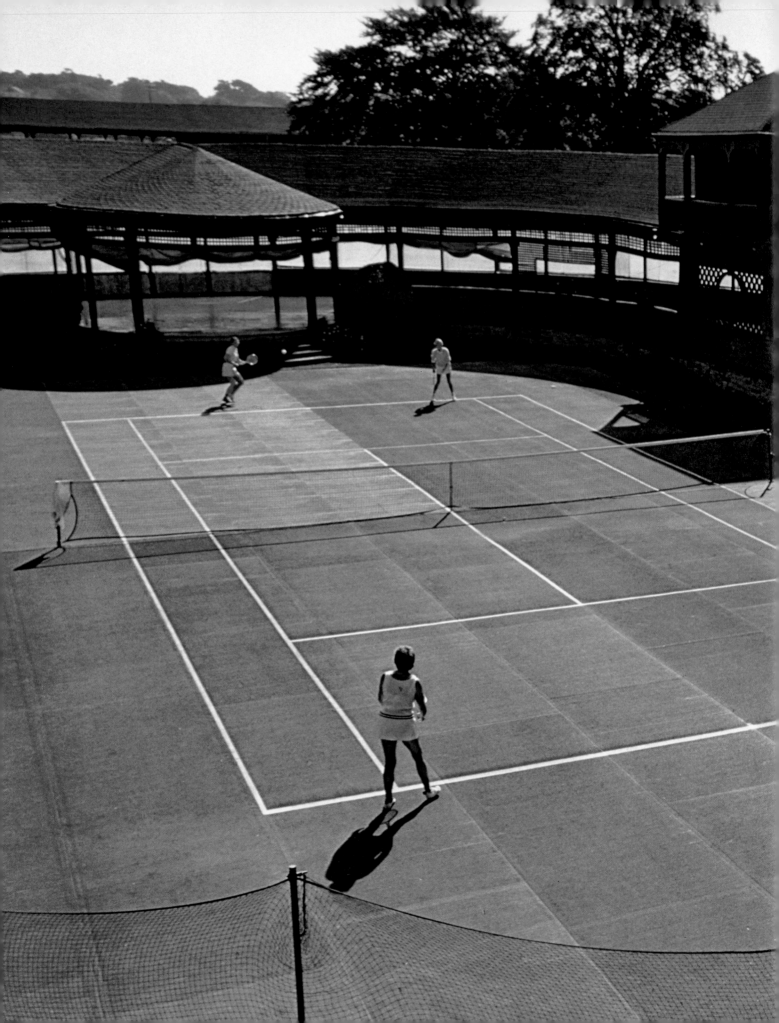

notes on an obsession

I have played tennis most of my life. On a few occasions —not always winning ones—I have played it well. Most of the time I have played it erratically, ineptly, frustratingly. Or, to put the matter more honestly than I'd like, downright badly. But I have never played it indifferently and I have never turned down a chance to play. I have played when I should have been writing, when I should have been entertaining or instructing my kids, or just keeping off the ankle I sprained landing awkwardly after a rather glamorous leaping overhead at the net. If the phone rang right now and someone offered me a game, believe me, I'd leave this sentence unfinished and . . . I mean, it's pleasant enough to be paid to write about tennis (something no one has thought to do until now), but it is nothing compared to the pleasure of a friendly hit. Or, for that matter, an unfriendly hit.

Obviously, you have not put yourself in the hands of an expert here. I wouldn't presume to tell you how to improve your backhand or sharpen your volley, or anything useful like that. Rather, you're mixed up with someone very like yourself, someone possessed of a major passion and an exceedingly minor skill for the game. Yet if, as the surveys tell us, thirty million Americans are playing the game, it stands to reason that the vast majority of that vast minority is composed of people I could give a decent game to, thus can, perhaps, give a decent book to. I say this out of the conviction that the questions which naturally occur to me as I look over the exponentially expanding world of tennis must be similar to those that occur to all other devoted amateurs of the sport, and that my answers probably come pretty close to those of any other tennis freak were he offered the time and the incentive to ponder our shared situation.

The most obvious of these questions is whether or not our little world can withstand the effects of the population explosion that has been visited upon it in the last decade or so. It is a question, after all, that is presented to us nearly every time we play. Here we are, warming up for a match at midnight because that's the only available time we can afford at our nearest "indoor facility" (which, likely as not, is an inflatable canvas bubble run up by someone whose fast-food franchise is now in bankruptcy proceedings). Here we are, stumbling out of bed at 6 a.m. in order to squeeze an extra hour at the public courts before they crowd up. Here we are, sitting on a sideline bench, cooling our heels (and feeling our muscles go stiff) while some kids, barefoot and wearing sawed-off jeans, bloopily try to teach themselves the game on a court they commandeered from us when our hour or our set (depending on the local rationing system) ran out. At such moments you can't help but feel a certain nostalgia for the good old days—all of eight or nine years ago—when you could always get a court and could play on it until you dropped.

Nor are crowds our only woe. There is the nature of the people who compose the crowds to contend with. Having finally gained access to the sacred seventy-eight by twenty-seven foot rectangle—such an elegantly simple bit of geometry—there is a better-than-even chance that the adjoining court will be occupied by four ladies exchanging hints on the latest supermarket specials between languid rallies. Or by a pair of hard-charging businessmen who have brought their noisily overachieving style —and ethical sense—directly from work to play. Or by a pair of transactional therapists employing the wiles of their craft not on their patients but one another. (One of these characters dominates the courts at Seaview, Fire Island, by the simple expedient of setting his watch fifteen minutes fast and marching onto your court, pointing to its face, and ordering you hence. He is a rather imposing figure, but more important the authoritative mantle of his profession is draped invisibly over his Lacoste shirt and I have never heard anyone dispute him about the time of day.)

To be sure, many of these people are innocents about the niceties of tennis's traditional politesse. And some, of course, are driven to ignore tradition by the exigencies of a day in which there are simply not enough courts, and not enough hours in the day, to accommodate all the newborn players. The former are occasionally educable and the latter couldn't be sorrier (guiltier is probably a better word) about their transgressions. But what are you going to do when the democratization of the sport has

Opening pages: Foursome plays a
lively match under optimum conditions
on Henry Heffernan Memorial Court
at Newport (RI) Casino. Playing
area is spacious, all-weather surface
well tended, possession of court
total and unthreatened, and
concentration is complete Casino,
home of Tennis Hall of Fame,
is a Newport landmark architected
by McKim, Mead & White.
Below: "Excellence . . . is always
within tantalizing reach."

13

Space is where you find it.
Bulbously curved bubbles
nestling under Queensborough
Bridge offer indoor
clay courts and circumscribed
playing area in overcrowded
Manhattan. Rumble and
gear-shifting of bridge
traffic overhead and street
traffic outside seem to
reach crescendo as
Schickel's service toss
reaches its crucial apex.

occurred so suddenly that marketing experts inform us it will require a decade for manufacturers to expand their capacity to the point where they can readily supply an expanding "market" (the very term seems out of place in a discussion of tennis) with the basic equipment it requires—rackets and balls?

All of this inspires a gloomy wistfulness for the deserted courts of a very recent yesteryear—when it doesn't inspire glorious dreams of the ultimate tennis consumerism, a court of one's own, liberally posted with "Keep Out" signs and costing a minimum of $20,000 to lay down. Worse, perhaps, are the panicky speculations about how democratization could conceivably attack the essence of the game.

Here one speaks very subjectively, but the heart of the game's appeal, for me, at least, lies in the way its extraordinarily rational design, rules, traditions—its artfully simple stylizations and conventions—provide a reasonable framework—a set of ideals, if you will—that tame and discipline our sometimes lunatic, often comic efforts to master it. They give it, if I may risk a large phrase, a moral dimension.

This is a matter to which I will return in greater detail at several points in this narrative, but let me try to put it as simply as I can here at the outset. Aside from boxing, which is not much of a participant sport and, nowadays, not much of a spectator sport, either, it is hard to think of any athletic endeavor that takes place within a more intimate and uncomplicated playing area. Nor, when you come right down to it, are the basic techniques of the game very complex—in theory. The areas of attack and defense are small, the largest "team" you can field consists of two people, and these factors minimize both tactical and strategic questions. Nor is there a vast variety of techniques to master. One must, of course, have a decent serve, a reliable forehand and backhand, and some ability to come to the net and volley. A cunning lob and an overhead of some ferocity complete the arsenal a tennis player requires. As the years go on he should develop a useful variety of speeds and spins to apply to these strokes.

Excellence in these skills is always within tantalizing reach; indeed, all of us attain it from time to time. In the midst of absorbing the most awful drubbing we somehow manage to surprise ourself (and our opponent) with an absolutely brilliant running backhand. Or put up a desperation lob that falls neatly, ungettably, bang on his baseline. Or angle a crisp volley cross-court that leaves him flatfooted. At such moments we know—not in our bones, but in our muscles, where it counts—that we could, dammit, beat the guy who has been savaging us. We know, too, that though we will never be a Laver or Billie Jean, we have it within ourselves to become a perfectly respectable player at our chosen level, that, indeed, we may even reasonably aspire to some slightly more elevated step on the club tennis ladder. What we need to acquire is consistency—the ability to make winners not in isolated splendor, but at a steady, reliable rate. We understand that this is a matter of practice and concentration, the ability to foresake all else when we step out onto the court, to permit nothing to intrude on the perfection of our relationship with the ball spinning toward us and our intentions regarding its flight off our racket. The legendary Bill Tilden was fond of repeating variants on the dictum that a tennis ball has no will of its own, that it can do nothing we do not tell it to do, and that all of tennis comes down to the simple matter of firmly giving it the proper instructions.

Here, of course, is where irony enters. Set aside for the moment the wit of our opponent's instructions to the ball, and the power with which he has imparted them, which may be, on the best day we ever lived, more than we can cope with. Let us also set aside for the moment such temporary inconveniences as the fact that we are out of breath from the last rally, that the calf muscle we pulled last week is tightening up, and that we are feeling twinges of incipient tennis elbow. Let us even refuse to consider that the shot required of us in this situation is (a) one we've been having trouble with all day for some reason, and (b) will place the ball exactly where he seems to want it. The thing to do, of course, is stroke it firmly, relying on the fact that our friend across the net is only human, and thus has an

15

almost infinite capacity to screw up the easiest imaginable tennis shot—even the one he appears to be all set for and is positively inviting us to make. The point is to wipe out everything (including the game and set scores) and to concentrate on making this the best possible shot the immediate circumstances allow.

That, precisely, is where the conditions of play now prevalent in a tennis-mad time rise up to frustrate us. Tennis is becoming a dreadful hassle. Assuming you make time in a busy schedule to put in the hours required to bring your game to optimum level, is it possible to get a court when you can conveniently, comfortably use it at a cost that does not add economic pressures to all the others now surrounding the game? If you do manage to find this dream court is it going to be surrounded by rude, loud, inept souls who will endlessly intrude upon the psychological space you need to play well—that envelope of privacy and silence into which every serious player must try to seal himself so that he can respond to the fierce demands the game places on his concentration? The chances are good to excellent that the envelope will somehow be torn asunder nearly every time the average citizen, the man who cannot afford the amenities of a well-designed private club, tries to play.

Here again I'm going to assume that my experiences are fairly typical. The courts nearest me in New York City are in Central Park. Just to sign up for a paltry hour you must make a special, early morning trip to the courts (no phone reservations accepted), confront a formidable line which eventually leads you into the presence of a formidable lady—the Gorgon of the facility—who seems to take perverse pleasure in informing you that all the good, Har-tru surfaces have been booked for the rest of the day, that the only thing she has available is one of the hummocky clay courts, and that only between six and seven p.m., which means agreeing to share the homeward walk through the park woods with the early-bird muggers. Still, a tennis court is a tennis court—not a thing to be lightly refused in New York City—so you sign up and tender your permit, which must have a passport photo affixed to it, for punching.

That, however, is only the beginning. Reporting in a few minutes before your appointed hour, you are confronted with a milling mass of anxious humanity, nudging and jostling at the entrance, awaiting the whistle blast signifying the turn of the hour at which courts are surrendered and claimed. What this agitated moblet is doing is jockeying for positions that will bring some of them through the gates first, thus obtaining thirty or forty extra seconds of playing time. When the starting whistle blows they will think nothing of trotting right through courts whose occupants are desperately trying to squeeze one last point into their expiring hour. In the back of everyone's mind is a lively fear that somehow the record-keeping has gone awry, that the same court will have been assigned to two sets of players, a matter which can consume a quarter to a third of one's precious playing minutes to settle. Of course, like everything else in New York, the courts are built too close together, which means that errant balls from the courts adjoining yours are going to sail distractingly past you during many a rally. The chances also are excellent that some never-say-die type is going to come crashing into your playing area in pursuit of the impossible get. Naturally, by midsummer the clay is impossible—unwatered and unrolled—so that every shot is played in a choking cloud of dust. The chalk lines marking the court's boundaries are laid down according to the myopic whimsy of an anonymous Parks Department employee who seems to bring only one feeling to his task, namely class resentment. What secret joys he derives from imagining the swells arguing ins and outs over his squiggles one can only imagine.

Winter in Gotham brings other kinds of fun. One year we played in a bubble located beneath the Queensborough Bridge. The clay was pretty well maintained, but one risked a shoulder separation whenever one carelessly pursued a shot that bounced more than a couple feet beyond the baseline, that being where the back wall of the courts, which featured some very nasty lighting fixtures, was located. There were also trucks to contend with; they had the habit of downshifting to accommodate them-

selves to the upgrade of the roadway overhead just as one's service toss reached its crucial apex.

Another winter a friend who was a faculty member at a local college discovered that its dean was a tennis freak and had ordered a carpet court to be spread on his gym's floor each weekend. Time, often great gobs of it, was available there, since the college drew its student body largely from that segment of the city's population for whom stickball is the formative sport. The fact that a lob of any pretensions was likely to be lost in the gym's low-hanging rafters was only a modest inconvenience. The fact that the carpet came in sections and that hard play caused these sections to rumple like a bathroom throw rug and to sepa-

rate, turning the playing rectangle into a parallelogram, was a different matter. One warmed up here not by rallying, but by smoothing the intractably heavy rug and tugging its sections back into position, so that all sidelines and center lines actually matched up.

Well, one persists. Tennis players tend to be hardy obsessives and not without the ability to see a certain humor in the predicaments to which their obsession inevitably leads them. Yet, as writer John Underwood has observed, "One facet of the tennis boom is that it has the power to cloud men's minds so they cannot see," and one of the main things they can't see is that it is becoming increasingly rare, if not totally impossible, to play the game as it

Twelve of America's estimated
thirty million tennis
players display varieties
of stance, form, and effort.
"The legendary Bill
Tilden was fond of repeating
. . . that a tennis ball has
no will of its own, that it can
do nothing we do not tell
it to do, and that all
of tennis comes down to the
simple matter of firmly giving
it the proper instructions."

Drawing by Saxon; © 1971
The New Yorker Magazine, Inc.

June 19, 1971   THE   Price 50 cents
NEW YORKER

should be played, to savor the deepest pleasure the game has to offer—those days when we are mentally as well as physically fit to give ourselves over to the rhythms which the sweet inner logic of the game will dictate if we can but abandon the world in favor of those rhythms and that logic. Too much, these days, we arrive frazzled at the court, further fray ourselves as we get snagged on the impediment of securing a rectangle for ourselves, and finally snap because there is not enough time to warm up properly, to find the groove of our game.

This situation, of course, is made to order for those tense and eager businessmen who are intent on developing the tennis "market." For what, in effect, are they actually offering us but expensive shortcuts to that state of grace which could formerly be obtained by the simple expenditure of time, but which the advertisements now assure us can be obtained—in the widespread absence of that commodity—by making a bold backhand shot with our wallets? Do they really expect me to believe that if I pay $30 or $40 for sneakers they will add wings to my feet, cause my forty-two-year-old legs to magically regain the spring of ten and twenty years ago? Do they really imagine, desperate as I am for a better backhand, that I think a $145 graphite racket is going to make it three-and-a-half times better than the $40 (on sale) Wilson T-2000 that admirably follows my screwy instructions on that shot? Am I to believe that arriv-

19

ing at courtside with my gear packed in a $50 Gucci tennis bag is going to so uplift my morale or so demoralize my opponent's that it is worth the investment?

There are moments, of course, when I would dearly love to believe these pipe dreams, but I have been beaten by too many canny old gentlemen in their late sixties who think my steel racket is probably the devil's handiwork, whose sneakers are deplorably anonymous in construction, and who regard the Lacoste alligator on my tennis shirt as a certain signal they've got a patsy on their hands.

I am even wary, these days, of coaches. Years ago, when one of them taught me the rudiments of the game, tennis coaches were regarded as a rare—perhaps even endangered—species. It was understood that whatever their competence as teachers, they must be dedicated souls, since manifestly the rewards and the prestige involved in their work were extremely modest. There is nothing endangered about them now; indeed, there are probably not enough of them to go around. We have some two hundred tennis camps in the United States and though they may advertise the presence of one of the great touring pros, the man or woman who spends up to $500 a week for a crash improvement course at one of these places may well be taught by unbilled bit players in the great tennis drama, or be soothed by such gimmickry as closed-circuit television hook-ups which permit the player to see and study what's right and what's wrong with his game, which is presumably more educational than hearing the bad news from a second party, or just feeling it in your bones when a shot goes wrong.

If tennis camping strikes the well-heeled enthusiast as too monomaniacal an experience, he can check in with a pro who boasts some former competitive fame —or at least a national ranking—and who may deign to take his case for $50 an hour, which is approximately what a psychiatrist would charge to free him of his mania. This seems to me . . . well, excessive. On the other hand, one may actually get more for his money at this end of the instructional scale than at the other, where some character who

may or may not have made the lower echelons of his high-school tennis team will expect $10 or $20 an hour for repeating, rather spiritlessly, the endless, unvarying litany of routine coaching. ("Relax, keep your eye on the ball. Follow through. Remember your feet.")

For around the same price a number of pros offer basic instruction en masse, gathering anywhere from ten to a hundred scholars about them and putting them through the basic paces of the basic shots for an hour or so every week. A member of such a group may consider himself lucky if he actually gets to hit a single ball for every dollar he spends. And he could surely put his money to better use by simply using it to buy more playing time for himself. In any event, it is perfectly clear that since there are no official standards or licensing procedures for tennis pros, anybody with a tan, a dazzling smile, and a not-entirely-abrasive personality can set himself up in business. It is also a situation in which the buyer had better be extraordinarily wary.

But wariness is not a quality one sees much around tennis anymore. The game at the moment is too chic, too fashionable, too much the "in" thing to do. After almost a century of not expanding fast enough—considering what a basically appealing game it is—it is now, manifestly, expanding far too quickly. Anyone with enough interest in tennis to pick up this book knows why. Sometime in the late sixties it became apparent to television programmers that tennis might be a game they could inflate as they had professional golf and professional football. It is intimate, easy for the camera (and the audience) to follow, full of action and suspense, and—if some system for quickly breaking ties is employed—predictable, and not excessive in length. Its principal—and, in fact, only—problem was that there was not enough of it. There was no way to generate the kind of relentless exposure which had simply broken down whatever resistance existed in those other sports. And, alas, there was no money involved in the game—at least visibly. It was an open secret that the best players were paid under-the-table fees for gracing tournaments with their presence, but Americans seem to get really

worked up about a game only when there is money in sizable amounts openly riding on the outcome of play.

By this time, of course, considerable resentment had built up among the best players over what must have seemed to them a cruel form of exploitation, especially at this late date. In every other sport they saw players who had attained comparable levels of excellence receiving handsome rewards for their efforts. Only in tennis was an entirely artificial break imposed upon the athlete's career. He could turn pro after he had won Wimbledon or Forest Hills, or helped his country win or defend a Davis Cup. And he could make reasonable money by so doing, if he didn't mind joining a small traveling circus of players, doing one-night stands in municipal auditoriums, high-school gyms—anywhere that offered a flat surface and some seating capacity. The pros, however, were pariahs, barred from competing in the very tournaments that carried with them the most prestige and public interest, the very ones that had, in fact, made them pros in the first place. (The great Pancho Gonzales, in particular, was penalized by this system, spending the best years of his tennis life playing an endless, meaningless round-the-world series of matches with Tony Trabert, Lew Hoad, and Ken Rosewall, all of whom also should have been competing in the great traditional events.) What was particularly galling was that the so-called amateurs were that in name only. "Expenses" and per-diem allowances were so generous, especially abroad, that as Billie Jean King has said, "It was a standing joke that the foreign amateurs couldn't afford to turn pro because they'd have to take a cut in pay." Arthur Ashe once said, "We all deserve Oscars for impersonating amateurs."

Open tennis was the obvious answer, as it had long since proved to be for golf, and sensible people had been advocating it since the 1920s, when Tilden and Lenglen and the rest had begun the process of converting tennis from a country-club sport to a generally popular (if not quite mass) entertainment. The reason "shamateurism" had persisted was quite simple: the game was an upper-class amusement and, although the majority of its great stars were anything but highborn, organizational control of the sport had remained with the well-to-do. They understood that open tennis would dilute their authority.

By the late sixties, however, so many of the great players—Rod Laver and Ms. King among them—had turned pro that tournaments like Forest Hills had become jokes. Everyone knew that a very large percentage of the best players were not present, that victories in these and the other major national championships were, very simply, tainted. And they were not, as a result, good show biz from television's point of view.

So, here were restless players, tired of the hypocrisy of the situation, and restive broadcasters, tantalizingly close to having a very marketable product, both frustrated by a small group of willful old fuds who had no reasonable defense for clinging to their reactionary ways. What tennis needed was an infusion of capital and some sporty entrepreneurs who could convert professional tennis from the catch-as-catch-can shambles it had been into a stable, attractive institution—a way of life, if you will—that would attract a sizable majority of the seasoned competitors away from shamateurism.

As it happened, neither was hard to find. By the late sixties a new breed—men who had found pleasure and profit and social prestige in organizing new franchises in the major spectator sports—began looking into the possibilities of tennis. Many of them were from the so-called sun belt—Florida, Texas, California—where they had made fresh new money in oil, aerospace, electronics. Tennis was much played in these regions and they had produced most of America's fine players in the postwar years. Moreover, they had a natural antipathy to the old-money easterners who controlled the United States Lawn Tennis Association. These newcomers could easily be persuaded to organize a series of professional tournaments, and one of them —Lamar Hunt—would shortly organize World Championship Tennis, signing most of the era's major players to professional contracts and setting them to playing a series of highly profitable tournaments on an almost weekly basis throughout the winter. Besides these people there were corporate executives all over the world who saw a chance to

Instruction is big business.
Tennis camps abound,
offer staff and facilities
for every level of competence
from young beginners
(bottom) to relatively able
adults (below & r).
Students may struggle
anonymously in large class,
get professional analysis
while watching self on video
replay, or even exchange
hits with Rod Laver.

enhance their products' images by associating them with this increasingly fashionable game.

In the event, the mere threat of activity by these people proved sufficient. To its infinite credit, the most ancient and honorable of all the major tournaments, Wimbledon, perceived the handwriting on the wall first. In 1968 it became an open tournament, offering cash prizes of increasing amounts as players moved through the draw to the championship. The rest of tennis quickly fell into line, though squabbling between competing fiefdoms persists to this day—a puzzlement to the public and an annoyance, too, since what appear to be in dispute are not principles but personalities whose feuds are indecipherable to those outside the little world of big-time tennis.

Be that as it may, the deluge has followed. It is now theoretically possible for a top-ranked professional to play in some tournament somewhere just about every week in the year. It is routine for at least a half-dozen players to make more than $100,000 in prize money alone, and routine for the majority of the list of big winners to be made up of names that are anything but of the household variety—guys who make the quarters and the semis of major tournaments from time to time, and win once or twice at one of the more obscure stops on the WCT tour. There is no question, among the pros, that there are more than enough good players available to fill out the draw at important tournaments. It is no longer possible for the top seeds to coast through the early rounds of a major national tournament. The possibility of an upset is now, as was not the case heretofore, omnipresent. On the other hand, the feeling persists that, just as it is with the humble weekend player, distractions may be distorting and diluting many of the best games in the game.

To be sure, these distractions are of a different

character than those from which the rest of us suffer in our quest for reasonable amounts of playing time in pleasant surroundings, but they have the same effect. If a player is bouncing from tournament to tournament in a perpetual state of jet lag, if he is under constant pressure from business demands (endorsements to attend to, the investment in the tennis camp to be overseen, the high-priced exhibition to be played), he cannot be expected to play his best. Indeed, if he were to ignore all this and simply concentrate on his tournament career, he would still not be a consistent winner, simply because no one can successfully play as much tennis as the modern pro is tempted to play and play it well. Jack Kramer theorizes that if a top-ten pro wants to bat more than around .250 (that is, win more than a quarter of the tournaments he enters), he ought to cut by two-thirds the number of invitations he accepts, which nowadays exceeds thirty a year on the average.

Such self-restraint, however, is difficult to practice. There is such good money to be made just getting to the round of sixteen repeatedly. Moreover, for players who began their careers as shamateurs, there is the temptation, after all those years of deprivation, to make as much money as they can out of the game before age catches up with them. It is difficult to blame them. If the former rulers of the game had made a gentle, well-managed transition to open tennis, if they had not had to be deposed by revolution, things might be different in tennis today. But basic political science teaches us that excesses always follow in the wake of a reactionary ruling class's violent overthrow, and those excesses are what tennis now must contend with. Such absurdities as team tennis with its one-set matches (in which substitutions are permitted) and its encouragement of cheering (and jeering) would never have occurred except in a post-revolutionary atmosphere. Neither would such weird happenings as the King-Riggs match, or the $100,000 winner-take-all match in a Las Vegas gambling casino between Rod Laver (cast against his true type as the game's grand old man) and Jimmy Connors, fulfilling an unprecedented role in tennis, that of the vulgar upstart, a permanent villain for crowds to actively root against. It might

even be that the tie-breaker, which television believes is required, but which players universally deplore and which distorts the game's ancient symmetry, might have been avoided had the growth of the game not been artificially held back for so many years, only to be artificially forced, as it now is, by commercialism and media hoopla.

That is, however, more speculation. We are dealing not with history as we wish it had developed, but as it actually has. And we would be less than honest if we confronted recent developments with anything but ambiguous feelings. For those of us who have loved the game as long as we can remember, it is undeniably pleasing to see so many converts, whatever their motives, whatever their style of attacking the game. It is always pleasant to feel that you were a prophet before your time, to see sizable numbers of people coming around to your way of thinking—even if it is only about a game.

If, on the other hand, one is concerned that the essence of the game cannot withstand this barbarous assault by the multitudes, one must coldly console oneself with the thought that it has somehow withstood neglect and mismanagement, that the elegant simplicity of its design probably betokens—as that quality does in other realms of life—great tensile strength. In one's more optimistic moods, one does remember that tennis is more than a faddish fancy, that its sheer difficulty will drive away those who think of it as only a game, a pleasant diversion that permits one to buy handsome clothes and to consume expensive gadgetry while encouraging a healthy tan. Tennis is, finally, an obsession or it is nothing. In the years to come, millions who are now dabbling in the game will decide it is nothing, that they are not willing to give the game what it demands before it will yield up its joys.

A smaller number of millions will, however, succumb to it, will join the great fraternity of players. Those a sensibly growing game can and will absorb, and benefit from at every level of participation. They—one imagines and hopes—will complete the process of democratizing the game without turning it into just another form of mass entertainment.

29

prehistoric times

The name and the game derive from the ancient net-and-racket sport known in France, where it was invented, as Jeu de Paume, in Britain—charmingly—as Real Tennis, in Australia as Royal Tennis, and in the United States as Court Tennis. This sport had its origins in the Middle Ages—it is mentioned in twelfth- and thirteenth-century manuscripts—and the four-walled court on which it is played is a stylized representation of a medieval courtyard. Our word, tennis, is generally assumed to be derived from the French *tenez!*, which, it is said, is the warning cry of the server to his opponent immediately prior to putting the Jeu-de-Paume ball into play.

Now, *tenez* is the imperative form of the verb *tenir*, meaning "to hold," and it in turn shares a Latin root with a word most experts agree is the prime requisite for the modern player—"tenacity." Certainly it is a quality much to be desired in the court-tennis player, since it is a fierce and maniacally complex game. Indeed, it was always regarded as the exclusive pastime "of noblemen to stir their body," as a seventeenth-century verse puts it. In part, of course, the game remained exclusively an aristocratic one because of the cost of building the court. (Today it is estimated that it would require $500,000 to run one up, which is why there are only seven of them in the United States.) But it also was believed that the game required—and encouraged the development of—virtues of character that one could not expect the lower orders to possess or need. In his list of "Courtly exercises and Gentlemanly pastimes" which "young men should use and delight in," Queen Elizabeth's tutor included "to ride comely: to run fair at tilt or ring: to play at all weapons: to shoot fair in bow, or surely in gun: to vault lustily: to run: to leap: to wrestle: to swim: to dance comely: to sing, and play of instruments cunningly: to hawk: to hunt" and last but not least "to play at tennis."

French kings were particularly enthusiastic about the game and two of them died as a result of that enthusiasm: Louis X of a chill he took after playing a rather energetic game, Charles VIII after being struck on the head by the very heavy ball then in use. (It was wool wrapped in leather.) Despite these catastrophes, their successors kept up the sport, and by the sixteenth century there were between two and three hundred Jeu-de-Paume courts in Paris alone and an estimated two thousand throughout the country. Indeed, François I, who reigned from 1515 to 1547, felt when he built his great flagship, *La Grande Françoise*, in order to outclass the *Great Harry* of England's Henry VIII, that a Jeu-de-Paume court was a necessity on board. Very likely his rival across the Channel regretted his omission of this convenience on the *Great Harry*, since in his younger days he was an ardent tennis buff "at which game it is the prettiest thing in the world to see him play," according to one of the ambassadors at his court. Indeed, during the sixteenth century there was not a first-class royal house in Europe that did not patronize the game.

By the next century, however, the game was in decline. In France the later Louis' were indifferent to it, while the English Puritans outlawed it along with all the other pleasures they could think of. It enjoyed a brief renaissance during the Restoration, but the Hanoverian kings of the eighteenth century were immune to its charms and, of course, the French revolutionaries had no use for such aristocratic fripperies, though they were responsible for the game's only mention in the mainstream of political history. Locked out of their normal meeting place by order of the king, the third estate of France met on the Jeu-de-Paume court at Versailles in 1789 and there swore the "tennis-court oath," vowing not to disband until their country had a constitution. By this time, however, there were only about a dozen such courts in Paris—there are now but two in all of France—and the game was on its way to its present status as one of our more curious bits of sporting exotica.

Nonetheless, we owe a great deal to the game by whatever name we call it.

The notion of hitting some sort of ball with some sort of stick seems to be a near-instinctive human urge. (Tennis historians are always trying, somewhat dubiously, to extend the game's lineage backward in time to stick-and-ball games played in ancient Greece and Persia.) So is

33

Shape and dimensions of
modern court-tennis playing
area appear to have
been established as early
as 1767, judging by
French Jeu-de-Paume court
below. Right: Manual
of same year offers guidance in
stringing rackets, winding
balls. Bottom: Outdoor
rackets court of mid-19th
century was roughly half of
today's tennis court.

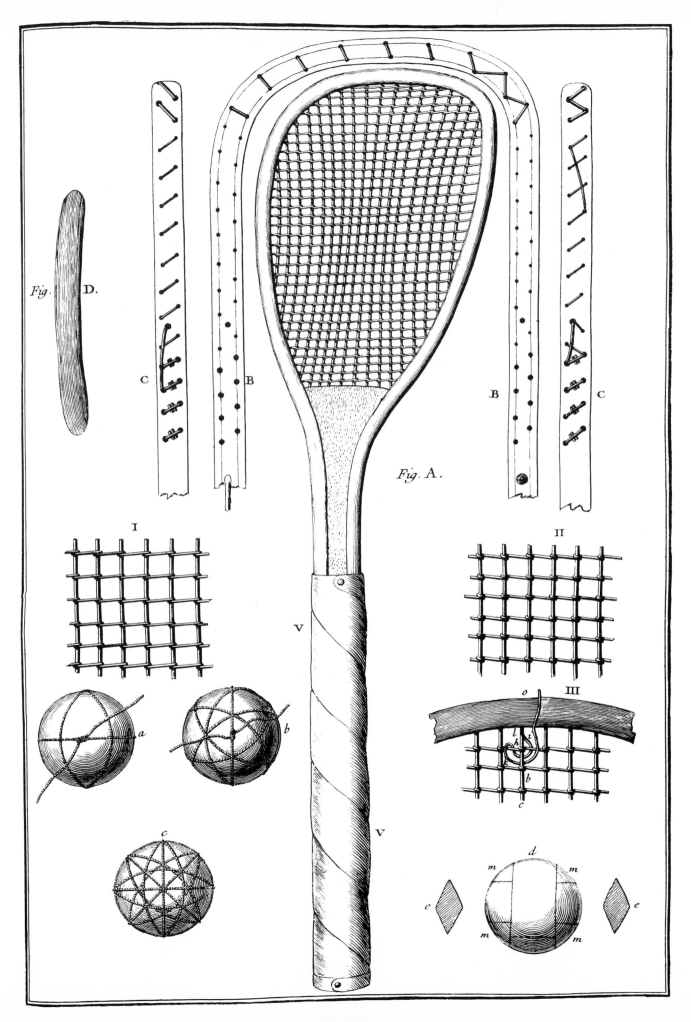

Fig. D.

C   B

Fig. A.

B   C

I

II

V

III

V

a   b

o

l t
h
k
b
c

c

d
m   m

e   e

m   m

35

the impulse to turn this atavistic muscular itch into some sort of contest. Jeu de Paume made two major contributions to the arsenal of equipment with which men could scratch the itch: the gut-strung racket, which adds an element of delicacy and refined control to our batting, and the net, which helps to make things really interesting as we slug away at each other.

The Court Tennis rackets, it should be noted, did not fall into disuse when the popularity of the game declined. Noble gentlemen in straitened circumstances often brought them along to the English debtors' prisons of the seventeenth and eighteenth centuries and used them to while away the time by batting balls against the walls. From this entertainment two fine games, rackets and (later) squash rackets, developed. In this same period efforts were made, here and there, to transfer Jeu de Paume outdoors, and in 1767 a game known as "field tennis" was played at a place called The Red House, in Battersea in England. Not much is known about it, except that the field itself was a fine lawn of the sort suitable for lawn bowling, and that mighty eating and drinking surrounded play. Fifteen years later the sporting press was still mentioning the game and

suggesting it had a certain popularity. Then, however, it simply disappears from the historical record.

One imagines that the main problem encountered by the devotees of field tennis was the ball, which must have been a variation of the Jeu-de-Paume ball. Obviously a sphere stuffed with wool does not have much bounce and required a hard floor and hard walls to make the most of its resiliency. In short, man's desire to bat ball with racket outside the confines of a walled, hard-surface court had to await the intervention of technology, and a century passed between the abortive invention of field tennis and the creation of a game something like modern tennis, for it was only in the latter part of the nineteenth century that that triumph of science, the hollow India-rubber ball, was placed stimulatingly before the public.

As early as 1858 a Major Harry Gem, a Birmingham solicitor, marked off on a lawn at suburban Edgbaston an outdoor court which dispensed with all the walls of Real Tennis but did retain, at least for a time, its court markings, which are radically different from those of lawn tennis. The game had considerable local popularity and in 1870 the courts were moved from Edgbaston to Leamington, the spa

Opposite: 16th-century court has heavily costumed players using short-handled rackets to hit ball over fringed rope, rather than net.
Left: Two gently curved court-tennis rackets of 1870s, with modern Bancroft. Book, first ever on a tennis-type game, is Italian, dates to 1555. Below: Jeu-de-Paume in France.
Following pages:
Modern court-tennis court, one of few in United States, at New York's Racquet and Tennis Club.

over Coventry way, where the world's first club devoted exclusively to tennis was founded by Gem and friends.

Meantime, the man generally acknowledged to be the prime inventor of the game as we know it, Major Walter Clopton Wingfield, a dandy, a spare-time creator of parlor amusements which he licensed to manufacturers, and a gentleman-at-arms at the court of Queen Victoria, was fooling around with a net-and-racket game that he played publicly for the first time with friends at Lansdowne House in London in 1869. The net on that occasion was but two feet high, a condition he radically rectified during experiments over the next four years. In December, 1873, the game he evolved and eventually patented under the name Sphairistike, a Greek neologism meaning, literally, ball and stick, was introduced "to the Party assembled at Nantclwyd [in Wales, across the way from Liverpool]." The Party, otherwise unspecified, was encouraged to bang a ball back and forth over a net four feet eight inches in height on a court eighteen feet shorter than that used today.

There were other radical differences between the Major's game and the one we play today. The court, for example, was shaped like an hourglass, nine feet narrower at the net than at the baseline, which was three feet longer than its modern counterpart. Service was from a small rectangle drawn at the center of the baseline and only the server could score (as in badminton and rackets). Game was 15 points, but a deuce was declared if the players were tied at 14, and two consecutive points were required to win.

Perhaps the most interesting thing about Wingfield's invention was the rapidity of its spread through the English upper classes. Less than two years after that assemblage at Nantclwyd, the Major was announcing in the fifth edition of his booklet explaining the game that sets of equipment, which sold for more than $25, had been purchased by eleven princes and princesses, seven dukes, fourteen marquises, three marchionesses, fifty-four earls, six countesses, one hundred and five viscounts, forty-one barons, forty-four ladies, forty-four honourables, five right honourables, and fifty-five barons and knights. According to Lance Tingay, the distinguished British tennis critic and historian, the major was a shrewd merchandiser, who knew how to take advantage of the Victorians' new-found and quickly developing ability to mass-produce consumer goods.

A little more than a year after Nantclwyd, an

37

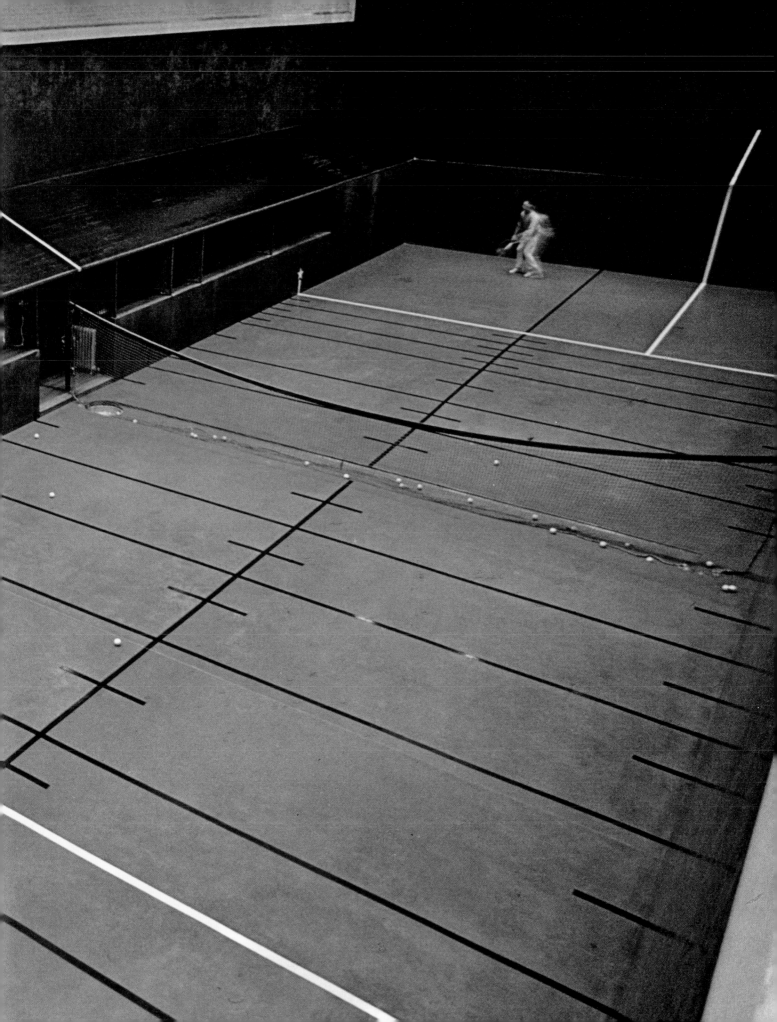

American woman named Mary Ewing Outerbridge, taking a winter vacation in Bermuda, observed British officers there playing a version of the game, bought a set of equipment to take home with her and, the following spring, aided by her brother, set up a court on the fine playing fields of the Staten Island Cricket and Baseball Club.

The same summer a court was also laid down in Nahant, Massachusetts, by one William Appleton. It is reported that the locals, hearing they were playing some sort of English game over at the Appletons, gathered round to watch, under the impression that what they were seeing was cricket. In less than a decade the new game was not only being played all over the world, there were national tournaments as well, especially in the English-speaking countries.

Indeed, interest in the game spread so quickly that less than a year after Wingfield's historic Welsh weekend, a committee of the Marlebone Cricket Club, the governing authority for the established sports of Real Tennis and rackets, convened to establish a standardized set of rules for the game—many players having used those tucked into their Sphairistike sets only as the roughest sort of guidelines for play. Wingfield's hourglass shape was retained, as was his basic scoring system. The service box, however, was eliminated in favor of a rule that merely insisted the server keep one foot behind the baseline, which was set at its modern distance of thirty-nine feet from the net. That obstacle became more formidable. It was five feet high at the posts, sloping down to four feet at the center of the court. However, the MCC committee proposed that the posts be seven feet in height so that cords could be stretched above the net. These were to serve as handicaps, the shots of expert players having to pass above them. The MCC committee was not, however, adamant about its handiwork. It suggested that players feel free to adapt the new rules to local conditions, and over at the Prince's Club in Knightsbridge they dropped the height of the net to its present standard of three feet at the center of the court.

More important, however, for the long-term history of the game were the financial difficulties afflicting the All England Croquet Club, located alongside the railroad tracks in the Worple Road at Wimbledon, in Surrey. It had come into being at the height of the croquet rage in 1869, but despite its handy location, just a few minutes outside London by train, it had not prospered and in 1875 one of the members, Henry Jones, proposed adding lawn tennis to the club's attractions. Two years thereafter, the club's prosperity had not improved sufficiently to meet the rising cost of ground rent, or to pay for the repair of the pony-powered roller for the grass. Again, Jones suggested that tennis might be the club's salvation. He proposed a men's singles tournament open to all comers. The editor of *The Field*, a sporting magazine, put up as a prize a silver challenge cup worth twenty-five guineas and so the greatest of all tennis tournaments was born.

Spencer W. Gore, the winner of that first tournament was, like many of the early lawn-tennis champions, a devotee of rackets who seemed to feel he was slumming when he played the new outdoor game. Some thirteen years after winning the first Wimbledon he remained unconvinced of its merits: "... it is want of variety that will prevent lawn tennis in its present form from taking rank among our great games. ... That anyone who has really played well at cricket, tennis, or even rackets, will ever seriously give his attention to lawn tennis, beyond showing himself a promising player, is extremely doubtful: for in all probability the monotony of the game as compared with the others would choke him off before he had time to excel in it."

That first Wimbledon had a significance beyond its status as the inaugural of a great tournament. Before opening day on July 9 (play continued through the twelfth, with a break for the weekend so as not to conflict with the Eton-Harrow cricket match at Lords), a committee met to determine rules of play and the results of their deliberations became the world standard. They decided to abandon Major Wingfield's scoring system in favor of that employed in Real Tennis, thus firmly linking their new game to an ancient and noble tradition. They also established the outer dimensions of the singles court at the measurements that

41

are still the regulation, though the service boxes have since shrunk five feet. There were a few other minor variations from the game as we now know it. The net was still five feet high at the posts, though it drooped to three feet three inches at the center; what would now be considered lets were played; and there were no advantage games. During the first years of competition, the first player to win six games took the set, even if his opponent had five. The ball, though roughly the same size as it now is, and made of rubber, was sewn together (cement-joined balls were not marketed until 1924), and the covering was white cloth, usually flannel, and not fuzzy in the modern style. Still, as far as one can tell, the ball bounced pretty much as ours does—a little slower, perhaps, but just as frequently frustratingly to its would-be master.

In 1880, when the Rev. J. T. Hartley won Wimbledon for the second consecutive year (the parson often disrupted the schedule when he played, since he had to preach on Sundays), the formerly moribund All England Croquet and Tennis Club, which had been used to showing profits in shillings and pence—if at all—netted (as it were) £230, the United States was holding its first open, and the final touches were being placed on the rules. At Wimbledon that year the net posts were lowered to four feet, a mere six inches higher than their modern height, the server was required to keep both feet behind the baseline, and the players changed sides at the end of each odd-numbered game. By this time, too, a men's doubles competition had been added to the tournament, though it would be another four years before women played at Wimbledon and not until 1913 that women's doubles and mixed doubles were added to the program.

As we look at drawings and photographs of competition in those days we are struck by the genteel air that seems to hang over the game: the gentlemen all in white and wearing long trousers (shorts were not worn at Wimbledon until the 1930s), their costume surmounted by cricket caps; the ladies wearing cumbersome skirts that reached to their shoe tops, starched white blouses and, more often than not, saucy boater hats. Most important, the attitudes the artists have captured seem generally to be without dynamism. There is nothing very tenacious-looking about these early players, who seem to have been convinced that the wristy stroke style of rackets and Real Tennis was as effective for the new game as it was for the older ones. Nor does the pictorial record suggest that they were playing with anything like the sweaty athleticism of tournament tennis as we now know it. The women, swathed in their long dresses, could not hope to move very frequently into the forecourt, and the early rulemakers seriously considered permitting the ball to bounce twice before women were required to hit it. In any event, as late as the teens of this century spectators at Wimbledon could remember the creak of stays punctuating the silence of Centre Court as the women strained for difficult gets. Indeed, it was not until after World War I that all world-class women players adopted the overhead serve, the feeling until then being that it placed too great a strain on all but the strongest of these allegedly gentle flowers.

Yet it may be that popular art plays us false, that there was more ferocity and power in early tennis than the antique costumery and gently phrased reminiscences lead us to think. For example, that first Wimbledon champion, Gore, was a noted exponent of the volley. He did not follow serve to net in the modern manner, but it was his wont to work his way up there as quickly as possible and, indeed, there was a lively controversy at the time over whether a stroke which ended with a player's racket over the net should be permitted. Eventually, of course, it was prohibited, and it was Gore they had primarily in mind when arguing the matter. One answer to that problem was provided as early as the second Wimbledon tournament, when P. F. Hadow, seeing the forbidding figure of Gore looming over the net, lofted a pretty lob which sent the defending champion scuttling back to the baseline, and eventually down to defeat—which may be one of the reasons he was thereafter so disparaging about tennis. Lobbers can make volleyers feel very glum about the game.

Around this time, too, it was beginning to occur, to the male players, anyway, that the serve could be some-

43

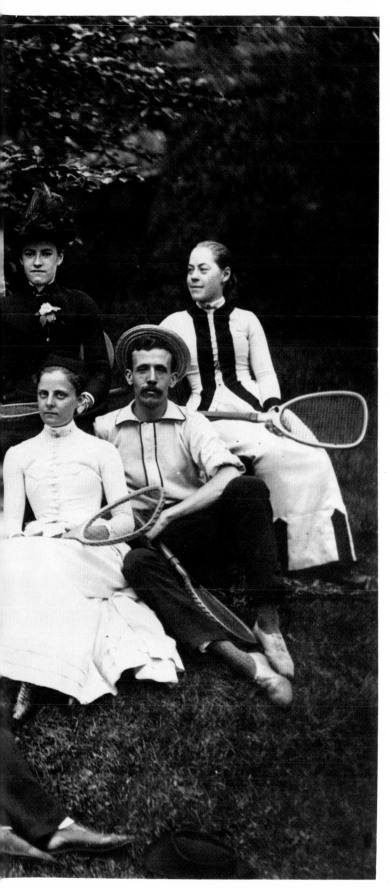

Group portrait by notable photographer Alice Austen (at left, with pug) was taken on "tennis ground" on a late August afternoon in 1886. In three years since Hayllar painting, design of racket has shifted to flatter top, more triangular shape. And young men in foreground appear to be wearing a sports shoe with rubber sole and no heel.

thing more than merely a means of putting the ball into play. (The name of the stroke, it is said, derives from its relative lack of importance in Real Tennis; Henry VIII and other royal enthusiasts literally employed a servant to toss the ball into play before each point.) Again, Gore was a leader in this development, his overhand serve being something of a sore point, particularly among the Real Tennis enthusiasts. They wanted the overhead banned because they believed it gave an unfair advantage to the server and because they sincerely believed lawn tennis should more closely ape their ancient game and be an exercise in the art of rallying. The debate did not last long. The first American championships, held in 1880, were won by O. E. Woodhouse, an Englishman, who shocked and amazed his hosts with his overhead serve, something the provincials had never seen before.

That same year Woodhouse and his "big game" reached the semifinals at Wimbledon, where he was put out by H. F. Lawford, a famously steady rallier, who was in turn put out by the Rev. Mr. John T. Hartley, also a groundstroke expert. But for the next decade Wimbledon was dominated by the Renshaw twins, the game's first truly famous players and first genuine attractions at the gate.

They had learned the game on asphalt courts at Oxford, and they came to it unhampered by the strategic preconceptions of the Real Tennis and rackets players, with their cut strokes and love of rallying. The Renshaws were just nineteen when they won the All-England doubles championships, which were staged at Oxford until moved to Wimbledon in 1884, a feat which they repeated six more times in that decade. "Both twins were powerfully built young men whose stamina was greater than that of most opponents they encountered," according to historian Alistair Revie. "They were also accomplished strategists and good stroke players. Willie possessed one of the earliest power-play services . . . and could also take the ball early with his ground strokes instead of on the drop. He was first rate at the net and sound overhead. Ernest was a more delicate and sensitive player, possessing most of the strokes and using them with a smoother and more graceful style."

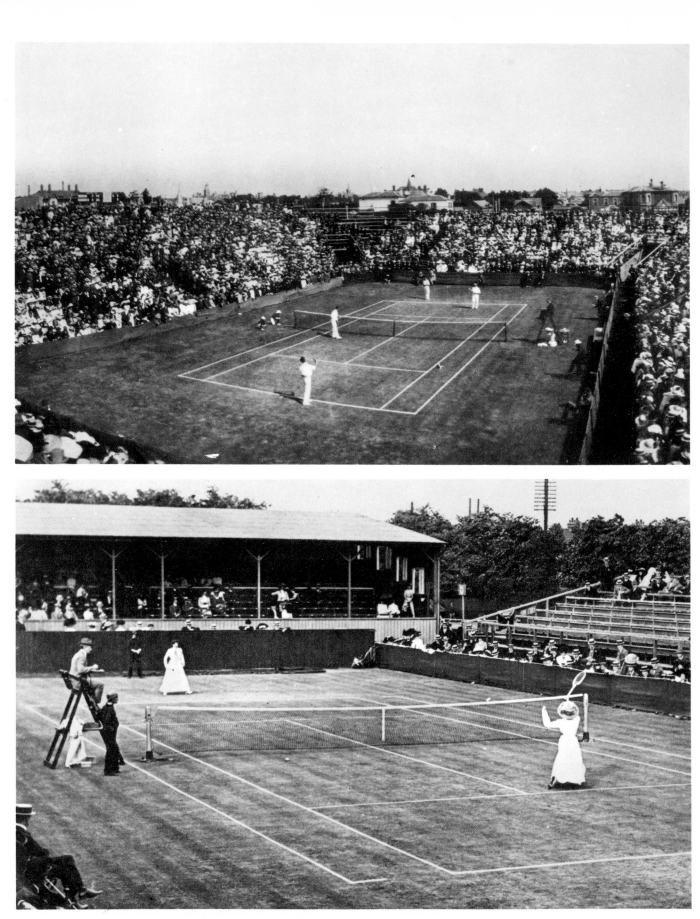

Alas for grace and style, the hustling Willie, with his famous "Renshaw smash," was by far the better player, winning six straight championships (1881–86) and adding the 1889 title. Smooth Ernest won only once, in 1888, and twice lost to his brother in the finals. In the entire history of the championships that comprise what we now think of as the Grand Slam (in addition to Wimbledon, it includes the Australian, the French, and the U.S. tournaments) only three players—all Americans (Richard Sears, William Larned, and Bill Tilden)—equalled his number of national titles.

The Renshaws, curiously enough, were not the only brother act in tennis during the game's formative years. They were almost immediately succeeded as perennial Wimbledon champions by the Baddeley twins, Wilfred and Herbert. The former was a three-time singles winner in the nineties, and as a team they won the doubles three times in the same period. They, in their turn, were succeeded by the Doherty brothers, R. F. (Reggie) and H. L. (Laurie), whose combined record, as the century turned, was superior to that of the Renshaws. The former won Wimbledon four times in succession during the years ending in 1900, the latter five times in the period 1902–06. They combined to win the doubles eight times during those years.

They were said not to have very "robust constitutions," and it is generally agreed that the competition at the top of the tennis world was not so strong as it was to become immediately after World War I. In those years, only Arthur Wentworth Gore, who won the title three times in the course of setting the record for most appearances at Wimbledon (he played from 1888 to 1927—thirty-nine times), a consistent quarter- and semifinalist named Sidney Smith, and, finally, Norman Brookes, the first of the great Australians, were in their class. Nevertheless, people who saw them and also saw the postwar greats felt that their "beautifully regular and severe" game could have been adapted to the more intensive style of play that marked the beginnings of the so-called modern era of the game, which is conveniently, and more or less accurately, dated by the arrival of Tilden at Wimbledon, when the tournament was resumed after the end of World War I.

How the Doherty brothers would have fared in that era is one of those questions that endlessly bemuse tennis historians, who seem to pass their winters by making up imaginary draws for a great tournament in the sky, at which appear all the champions from all the great tennis eras, magically restored to their prime and battling away on what must surely be the finest tennis lawn anyone ever conceived. What one can say for certain about the Dohertys was that they were the premier players of the era in which the game was internationalized. As early as 1883 two Americans (and yet another brother team), C. M. and J. S. Clark, reached the challenge round (or finals) of the Wimbledon doubles competition, and thereafter Americans more or less regularly appeared there. Indeed, the first non-British winner of a Wimbledon title was America's May Sutton, who won the women's singles in 1905, though not without some social difficulties, one of the English competitors objecting to the flash of ankle her tennis dress revealed and the bare forearms her short-sleeved blouse did not cover. Miss Sutton was not permitted on Centre Court until her hemline was lowered.

After her, the deluge. There were more entrants in the men's singles that year than ever before (seventy-one), and besides the United States, competitors representing Australia, Belgium, Denmark, New Zealand, Sweden, and South Africa appeared in the Worple Road for the festivities. Obviously, it would not be long before someone who was not a home-grown product would win the men's singles. That someone turned out to be the redoubtable Norman Brookes, who took the title in 1907 and again in 1914, when he wrested it from the graceful and popular Anthony Wilding, a New Zealander who had held it for four consecutive years and who, like so many of his generation, would die in the trenches in France the following year. The Brookes-Wilding match was the tournament's first entirely non-British final, beginning a tradition that would, in time, pass from exception to general rule.

Meantime, during these sunset years of the old order, English players were venturing forth to exotic

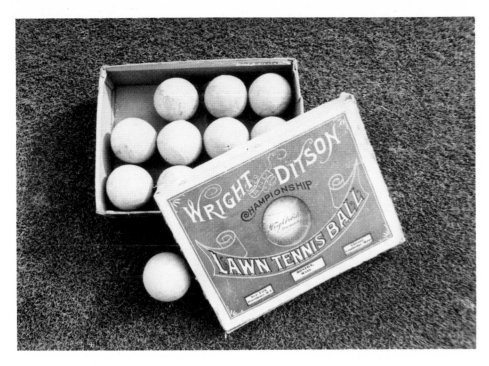

climes. The Dohertys, for instance, made the journey to Newport, Rhode Island, for the American championships, Reggie reaching the finals in 1902, Laurie winning the title the following summer. What brought the Dohertys across the sea, however, was not the thought of picking up some easy wins in a provincial championship, but the opportunity to participate, as representatives of their country, in the International Lawn Tennis Championships, better known as the Davis Cup and, over the years, the biggest single factor in creating world-wide interest in the game.

It all began with a modest proposal. In 1897, the U.S. Lawn Tennis Association suggested to its English counterpart that a team match between the two nations might be desirable. By 1900, when Dwight F. Davis, a player from St. Louis, agreed to donate a cup as prize—it was a solid silver punch bowl lined in gold and valued at $1,000—the regulations for the competition had been broadened so that any of the fourteen nations with a recognized LTA could enter. For the first four years, however, the Davis Cup matches were strictly an American-British affair, with the Yanks winning the first two trials in 1900 and 1902 (there was no challenge in the intervening year), largely because the Dohertys did not compete in the first matches and were misused in the second.

Indeed, the first Davis Cup encounter was something of a shock to the Englishmen. The competition was set for the Longwood Cricket Club outside Boston, and the British team landed in New York with only the vaguest sense of American geography. They made their way to The Hub by way of Buffalo, which is about the hardest way to go anywhere in the United States, and finally arrived in the midst of a heat wave. Temperatures were alleged to be as high as 136°F. They quickly discovered that the grass was twice as long as they had seen in England, that the balls were very bad—"animated egg plums," as one disgusted Englishman put it—especially when served in that wicked new manner known as the "American twist." The British managed to capture just one set in five matches, the one, ironically, from cup-donor Davis.

They fared a little better two years later, when the Dohertys took the doubles and Reggie managed to win one of his singles. However, Laurie, who had won Wimbledon earlier that year, was inexplicably held out of the singles and his substitute, Dr. Joshua Pim, could not cut it against William Larned, who won the U.S. title seven times in a career that history makes surprisingly little of, or against M. D. Whitman, a former U.S. titleholder. Perhaps the most interesting thing about this second cup competition was the crowd that turned out for the final day's doubles, played after the United States had clinched the prize. There were 10,000 in the stands that day, the largest assembly ever to watch a match up to that time and a tribute to the drawing power of the legendary Doherty combination.

Britain finally took the cup home in 1903, with a little help from the weather. The Dohertys were the entire British team this time, though a substitute was carried.

Reggie (I) and Laurie Doherty,
another pair of British brothers,
compiled a record superior even to
the Renshaws'. Reggie won
Wimbledon four times in a row, Laurie
five. Together they won doubles
eight times—all this in
decade 1897-1906. Their competition
could have been sneezed at,
but their performance
suggests that they would have
been as good as they had
to be against better players.

Suspense, however, developed when Reggie suffered an injury to his racket arm and the English nonplaying captain was informed that if he substituted for Reggie in the opening singles he would be forced to play the substitute in the second round of singles, as well. Remembering the fate of Pim, he ordered Reggie to default his opening match. Laurie then won his match, after which rain fell for two days, permitting Reggie's arm to heal. The brothers then won their doubles and, on the final day, both singles matches, though each was extended to five sets. The United States would not regain the cup until 1913, when Maurice McLoughlin, first of the great California players, and the game's first famous big server—he was known as "the Comet"—was in the side.

The British win was good not only for the national pride of the country which had invented the game, but for the Davis Cup competition in general, encouraging European nations to challenge for it in a venue nearer home. With Laurie Doherty a constant in the British side, the English retained the cup for three more years, while interest—in an increasingly nationalistic era—intensified all over Europe. It was, however, another English-speaking team which wrested the cup from the motherland and, until World War I intervened, dominated cup competition. It was a combined Australian and New Zealand team, competing under the name Australasia, which took the title five out of seven years between 1907 and 1914. That team, of course, was composed essentially of Norman Brookes and Tony Wilding, and they sent the cup Down Under for the last time in this era just four days after war began in August, 1914.

The war, of course, ended international competition and only the United States was able to keep its national tournament alive during the next four years, providing among other things a pleasantly isolated testing ground for "Big Bill" Tilden and "Little Bill" Johnston to sharpen the skills that would make the former the dominant player of the next tennis era, the latter his greatest native rival. It is, perhaps, a measure of how firmly the relatively new game had established itself that competition was so quickly resumed after the war—and at a new and higher level, at that. Only in revolutionary Russia, where it was associated with the idleness of aristocratic life, did it die out.

It must be admitted that in a certain sense, the commissars were right. Tennis may have spread in a little less than a half-century to every corner of the civilized globe and some corners of it that weren't so civilized. But it was thinly spread—a game for the well-to-do and the aristocratic. Their young men played it and their older men ruled it from the verandas of their clubhouses, the board rooms of their banks and businesses. Internationalism to them meant simply an opportunity to travel about the world and meet their opposite numbers. They did, to be sure, encourage the development of young talent, but they did not look far beyond their exclusive clubs for it. If they found a gifted player sprouting outside their walls, they felt it their duty to civilize him while pointing up his game, and even late in the modern age free spirits like Bobby Riggs, Pancho Gonzales, and Billie Jean King felt the power of their disapproval, usually expressed in minor discourtesies, unpleasant squabbles about expense money, and so on. In short, tennis began as a private preserve and the dialectic of its history is between those who were determined to keep it that way and those who were determined to force it to go public. What one cannot help but observe in these early years, however, is that the success of the Americans and the Australasians was bound to have, in the long run, a liberating effect on the game, for they were, unlike the other major tennis powers, meritocracies. The success of their nationals, whatever their social status, was bound to encourage eager young men to see in tennis a new road to the top and to take it up as a means of advancing their fortunes. It would take them a long, impatient time to change the shape of the game, to wrest effective control from the clubmen, but it must be recorded that the first seeds of revolution were planted in this prewar period of expansion. What the game required now were great personalities, star attractions who could command media attention and through it, the attention of the masses. They were waiting in the wings.

the first golden age

It is something like half a century since William Tatem Tilden II was at his peak, something like a quarter century since he died, broke and in disgrace, having served two prison terms—one for committing a homosexual act with a minor, the other for violating a parole that enjoined him from consorting with youngsters. Yet just days after he was released from jail the second time, which happened to be just days before this century turned fifty, an Associated Press poll of sportswriters voted him the greatest athlete in his sport by a margin larger than that achieved by any athlete in any other sport—a judgment from which no knowledgeable tennis authority cares publicly to dissent.

He compiled a wonderful record: seven U.S. singles championships, three Wimbledon singles championships, sixteen wins against just four losses in Davis Cup play, numberless other major titles in singles and in doubles (for which he claimed to have small aptitude). But it was not the number of championships he held that made Tilden the standard against which all other tennis players, including those who in his later years consistently beat him, are judged. It was the moment at which he accomplished his great feats, and the manner he brought to his conquests—and his defeats—which made him, make him, such a singular presence in tennis history.

His moment was that period that used to be known as The Golden Age of Sport—the age of Babe Ruth, Jack Dempsey, Red Grange, Notre Dame's Four Horsemen, and Bobby Jones, with all of whom Tilden stood as an equal. The period may not actually have been suffused with quite the glow nostalgia imparts to memory. None of the major sports was blessed with the depth of talent that has since become commonplace, and it seems likely that the modern athlete is both naturally stronger and the beneficiary of more sophisticated conditioning techniques. (The number of championship tennis matches in past eras that ended with the loser either collapsing or having to be helped from the court after a total expenditure of energy was astonishing.)

Yet the Golden Age was certainly the first in which promoters recognized that sports could be, inevitably would be, a big-money enterprise. It was also the first age in which it was recognized that excellence in a game was not enough, that it had to be combined with a public personality that could be exploited in order to capture the interest of the expanding mass media and their expanding audiences. If tennis had not had Tilden it would have had to invent him or it could not have held its own in the sports pages, in the talk of the nation, might never have developed the beginnings of the broad base of interest on which it currently rests.

Let me put the matter personally. I do not believe that my father, who was the first person to undertake the thankless task of teaching me the game, would have been a player had not the example of Tilden been placed before well-brought-up young men in the Middle West in the 1920s. Nor do I believe that there would have been places for us to play had Tilden not made people outside the country-club belt tennis-conscious. As it was, in the thirties and forties there were courts everywhere. A little farming community, a few miles from our vacation house, had two excellently maintained and rarely used courts to which we could repair for a hit any time we felt like it. Tilden, I firmly believe, was responsible for that fine, tree-shaded stretch of unpopulated asphalt in a place infinitely more interested in the price of corn and tobacco than it was in the USLTA rankings.

I doubt that Tilden ever knew or cared about this aspect of his influence; the evidence is that he was a remarkably shy, self-absorbed, and arrogant man. Yet even for those, like my father, who had never seen him play, he was the ideal incarnation of the tennis player, even the still photographs giving an impression, if not of how the game should be played, then how one should look while playing it. He was tall, slender, and graceful in his immaculate whites, endlessly captured by the camera in attitudes that suggested an effortless flow into position for shots of instruction-manual perfection. The press, the tennis world in general, did not let my father, or the rest of us, in on Tilden's secrets. His sexual proclivities were in that discreet age undiscussed, though there was evidently consid-

Opening pages
& left: Tilden in
1920s. In action
a study in
graceful
concentration.
In repose
betraying none
of his
inner turmoil.

erable fear among tennis's rulers that they might become public knowledge and hurt the game. Even such matters as his chain-smoking and his personal slovenliness (off court his clothing was unkempt and without style, and he often avoided the postgame shower because he hated to be seen naked in the locker room) were hushed up, as were the bad habits of other sporting figures who were ridiculously supposed to be setting an example for the nation's youth.

People saw in Tilden what they wanted and needed to see in the game's pre-eminent figure. They knew, for example, that he was a self-made tennis player (he had to be, since as late as 1914 there were only two teaching pros in the entire country), who had not been good enough to make the number-one spot on the tennis team at the small private prep school he attended in his native Philadelphia, or to make the varsity at Penn, which he quit before graduation. Then, however, tragedy struck the Tilden family. His excessively beloved mother died after a long illness in 1911; four years later his father and his older brother died within months of one another, driving Tilden into a deep depression that lasted for months. An aunt lectured him, telling him he must commit himself to something, anything, lest despondency come to rule his life. There were several things he cared about as much as tennis—music, for example, and bridge and the theater—but it was the sport to which he turned, perhaps because he saw in it a way of exercising some of his taste for the dramatic as well as his need for competitive challenge. Ranked seventeenth in the United States, he was put out of the first national championships he entered in the first round. Just two years later, in 1918, he reached the finals, where he lost. He lost again the following year, to "Little Bill" Johnston, largely because "Big Bill's" backhand was no more than a defensive weapon, not an instrument for attack. He passed the winter at the home of a friend who had one of the nation's few indoor tennis courts, working, working, working on his backhand.

In 1920 he went off to Wimbledon and became the first American to win the men's singles title there, defeating the Australian defending champion, Gerald Pat-

terson, with an astonishing bit of gamesmanship. Patterson was known to have a powerful forehand and a feeble backhand, which everyone attacked. In the first set, Tilden disdained it, slamming away at Patterson's forehand, losing the set 6-2. In so doing, however, he was able to study everything the champion could do with his best shot, come to the conclusion that thereafter he—Tilden—could handle it. Patterson thereafter had only weakness—his backhand—to fall back on and Tilden swept the next three sets.

A little later it was time to revenge himself on Johnston. It required five sets to do so, in a match played in the rain and interrupted by a midair plane crash in which two military pilots lost their lives. The accounts of the game insist that it was Tilden's powerful serve which finally broke the game little man, who had to be assisted from the court after the match, but one has the feeling that Tilden was toying with his opponent, blasting him off the court in the first set, deliberately losing the second, staging a dramatic comeback to take the third, then throwing away the fourth when he needed but two points for the match, thus setting up the 6-3, fifth-set crusher. Ever after, Johnston was unable to take a significant match from Tilden.

It all fits. In his memoirs Tilden wrote of the game as he had found it: "They played with an air of elegance—a peculiar courtly grace that seemed to rob the game of its thrills. . . . There was a sort of inhumanity about it." He added: "I believed the game deserved something more vital and fundamental." This was true, as far as it went, but Tilden added more than vitality to the game. What he contributed to it was ferocity. Sometimes, of course, just for the fun of it, or for dramatic effect, he extended a match he should have closed out in straight sets. On one well-known occasion, seeing that he had his opponent hopelessly outclassed, he began offering up the shots this poor soul had shown himself best able to return. Meantime, he began storming at umpire and linesmen until he had worked the crowd into an ugly anti-Tilden mood. At which point he finished the match off briskly and apologized to the official in the chair, H. LeVan Richards: "I'm sorry, Lev. I apologize. But they really deserved a show

59

The Four Musketeers. It took a
whole team of Frenchmen to bring down
Tilden (and teammate Johnston)
in the Davis Cup, and they needed three
tries (1925-27) to do it. Clockwise,
they are Jean Borotra, wearing his inevitable
beret; Henri Cochet, practicing his
notoriously weak backhand; René Lacoste,
whose frail constitution forced
his retirement from the game at 25; "Toto"
Brugnon, cheerful doubles expert. French
successfully defended the cup five
times, losing finally to Britain in 1933.

didn't they?"

More often than not, however, his efforts were directed toward devastating the man across the net, establishing a psychological superiority that would extend beyond the day's match, haunt the fellow down the years in tournament after tournament. Sometimes he would contemptuously pick up, say, four balls, fire the three aces he needed to finish the match, then grandly toss the remaining ball aside as he strode off the court. With Johnston, the next time they met in the U.S. tournament (it was a quarterfinal match) he decided to do without the big serve that everyone had said was the only part of his game that was decidedly superior to "Little Bill's." He beat him trading forehand baseline drives in a game of long rallies. That point settled, Tilden got into a real slugging match with the Californian in the 1922 finals. He let the first two sets get away from him rather easily, much to the delight of the crowd and the assembled officialdom of the USLTA, who by this time had wearied of Tilden's arrogance and his seemingly endless winning streak. He dropped three more games in the third set, then won six consecutive games to turn it—and the match—around. In the locker room afterward, it is said, Johnston was a broken man.

The word now was that Tilden could beat the smaller man only in endurance contests, that he deliberately extended their matches to five sets in order to wear down the frail Johnston. Stung by that criticism, Tilden in the next year's finals came out firing his powerful serve and wiped Johnston out in straight sets. They would meet in one more final, in 1925, and again Tilden would win in a long match, but by that time the truth of the matter must have been clear to the dead-game Johnston: Tilden had deliberately established his superiority in every kind of match, under every sort of condition, and there was simply no way for "Little Bill" to beat his arch-rival.

It should be emphasized, in the age of Jimmy Connors, that ferocity did not imply viciousness. There were many players who detested Tilden, principally for his inability to tolerate debate over his pronouncements about how the game should be played, for the way he dominated any room he entered, but it was never said that he was anything but a perfect sportsman on court. "Peach!" he would cry when delighted by an opponent's excellent winner, and he was famous for giving up the next point when he felt a linesman's error had done the man across the net out of a point. In 1922, when both Tilden and Johnston had won the U.S. title twice and were playing for permanent possession of the cup that was supposed to be the only tangible reward for winning, Johnston wearily told his nemesis after the match, "If I can't have the cup myself, I would prefer you of all men to have it." It may indeed be that Tilden won his second Wimbledon because he was such a fine—or at least self-consciously showy—sportsman. His opponent was B. I. C. Norton of South Africa, who found himself serving for match point. Tilden returned deep, thought it was out, and came chugging up to the net to congratulate Norton. The shot, however, was in. Norton thought Tilden was charging to volley and flubbed his return. Tilden went on to win the last set 7-5.

Such is the stuff from which legends are woven. Some, indeed, say that Norton was so impressed by Tilden that he threwe the match, unwilling to take the Wimbledon title from a man who was known to be sick, who had spent the week prior to defending his title in a nursing home. Be that as it may, even legends age and Tilden, who had come to greatness rather late (he was twenty-seven before winning a major title), would in the last half of "his" decade prove vulnerable to that remarkable group of Frenchmen known as the Musketeers—Jean Borotra, Henri Cochet and René Lacoste, and their quietly efficient fourth, Jacques "Toto" Brugnon, who played expert doubles. It took all of them to end Tilden's domination of the game, and only one of them, Cochet, appears to have established a definitive psychological edge on the American, although that too is open to debate.

Borotra, "the Bounding Basque" of the sportswriters' leads, was the most colorful of the group. He generally wore a cocky beret and generally came to the net after serving—the first major player to do so. A stylist of flash and dash, he had learned the game while vacationing in

First French assault on the Davis Cup. Left: Tilden and Borotra before their opening-round match. Below: The match in progress, at Germantown Cricket Club, near Philadelphia, which was Tilden's home ground. Despite this advantage, the "Bounding Basque" extended him to five sets before succumbing. In that first of eight consecutive meetings between the two nations for the cup, France did not win a match. Right: A good example of the Basque's bound.

England as a child, catching on to its intricacies after perhaps a day of instruction, helped by the fact that he had played pelota, the handball game native to his region. Cochet was a cheerful, lazy-seeming sometime ballboy, weak of serve and backhand, but possessed of an uncanny ability to take shots on the rise—the best way of turning an opponent's power back on him—and particularly demoralizing, for some reason, to Tilden. Lacoste was the son of a wealthy industrialist, had a frail constitution, and was forced to virtually retire from the game when he was only twenty-five. Until then he was famous for keeping a book on other players, noting strengths, weaknesses, and their propensities for certain shots in certain situations.

They began competing at Wimbledon in 1922, the year the old challenge-round system—in which the defending champion was not forced to defend his title until the final (or "challenge") round—was abandoned, and G. L. Patterson regained the title he had lost to Tilden. The Frenchmen did a little better the next year, when the All England Club abandoned its old grounds in the Worple Road and moved to its present site in Church Street, though "Little Bill" Johnston gained his only Wimbledon title that year, with Tilden absent. It was not until the following year's "fortnight"—1924—that Borotra, who often commuted from his job in Paris to Wimbledon by plane, began a great French winning streak—six straight Wimbledon championships—by taking the title from Lacoste in the first all-French final round.

The following year they met again in the finals and this time the results were reversed. It was obvious that the French were coming on. In 1925 and '26 they reached the Davis Cup challenge round and were set down by the Tilden-Johnston duo 5-0 and 4-1, Lacoste administering Tilden's first defeat in cup competition at the second meeting. Cochet, volleying with deadly effectiveness, also managed to put Tilden out of Forest Hills in the quarterfinals in 1926, and it was clear that the following summer would bring to a crisis the question of American leadership in international tennis.

Things began well enough for Tilden. He de-

feated Cochet in the French semifinals and lost to Lacoste in the finals in a five-set, three-hour match in which it appeared that Tilden had actually won when he seemed to have aced Lacoste on match point at 9-8 in the final set. The serve was called out, however. Lacoste steadied and went on to win the deciding set 11-9.

Tilden met Cochet again in the semifinals at Wimbledon and was blowing the young Frenchman off the court, leading 6-2, 6-4, and 5-1 in the third set when, suddenly, "Big Bill" lost seventeen points in a row and the set 7-5. He promptly lost the next two sets 6-4, 6-3. The umpire, an eighteen-year Wimbledon veteran, called the turnabout "the most astonishing event that has happened in my time at Wimbledon," especially since many who saw the match believed that the first two-and-a-half sets may have been the finest tennis Tilden ever played.

There were a dozen theories as to what had gone wrong. Tilden declared that Cochet, with his back against the wall, had simply risen to heights Tilden could not match. Others said Tilden tanked the match so that Cochet would be chosen for Davis Cup play where Tilden could then gain dramatic revenge. Others say the entrance of King Alfonso of Spain into the royal box just as Tilden was on the verge of victory distracted him—or perhaps encouraged him to extend the match an extra set in order to treat His Majesty to some first-class tennis. Others say Tilden was simply too tired to go five sets against his younger opponent, though the day was a cool one and Tilden went on to win plenty of long matches in the years to come. Given his love of drama and his supreme confidence, it seems likely that Tilden did let up just a little—lost his edge and never regained it, even as you and I do when we permit self-satisfaction to outrun common sense on days when for a time we seem miraculously able to do no wrong. Whatever happened, Cochet gained not only an important win (he went on to defeat Borotra in the final), but a career-long hoodoo on Tilden, who only rarely took him in important matches thereafter.

Now events began to conspire to produce what was perhaps the most dramatic of all Davis Cup competi-

In twilight of Tilden's career, Americans often were beaten by the Musketeers and the emerging British, but scored splendidly in doubles. Left: Four feet off the ground are Wilmer Allison (l) and everybody's favorite partner, John Van Ryn, winning from Borotra and Cochet during 1929 loss of Davis Cup to France. Below: George Lott (r) and Van Ryn topping Cochet and Brugnon to win at Wimbledon in 1931.

The French On the Rise. Below:
Cochet (rear) defeats Tilden in the
quarterfinals at Forest Hills
in 1925. Tilden had a bad knee that day,
but Cochet's long-run record against.
him was excellent—his ability
to take hard-hit balls on the rise
being particularly disconcerting
to the American. Right: One of
Tilden's few moments of revenge—a
four-set victory over Cochet
in the 1926 Davis Cup challenge
round, again at Germantown.

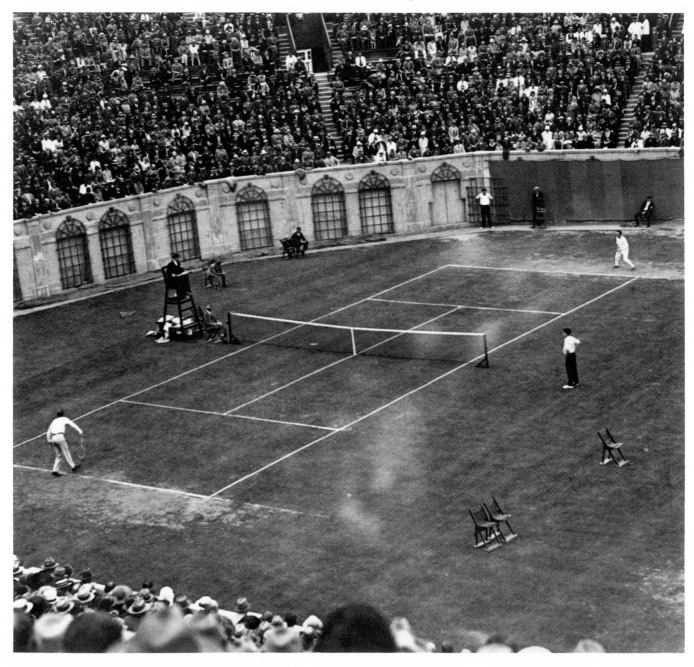

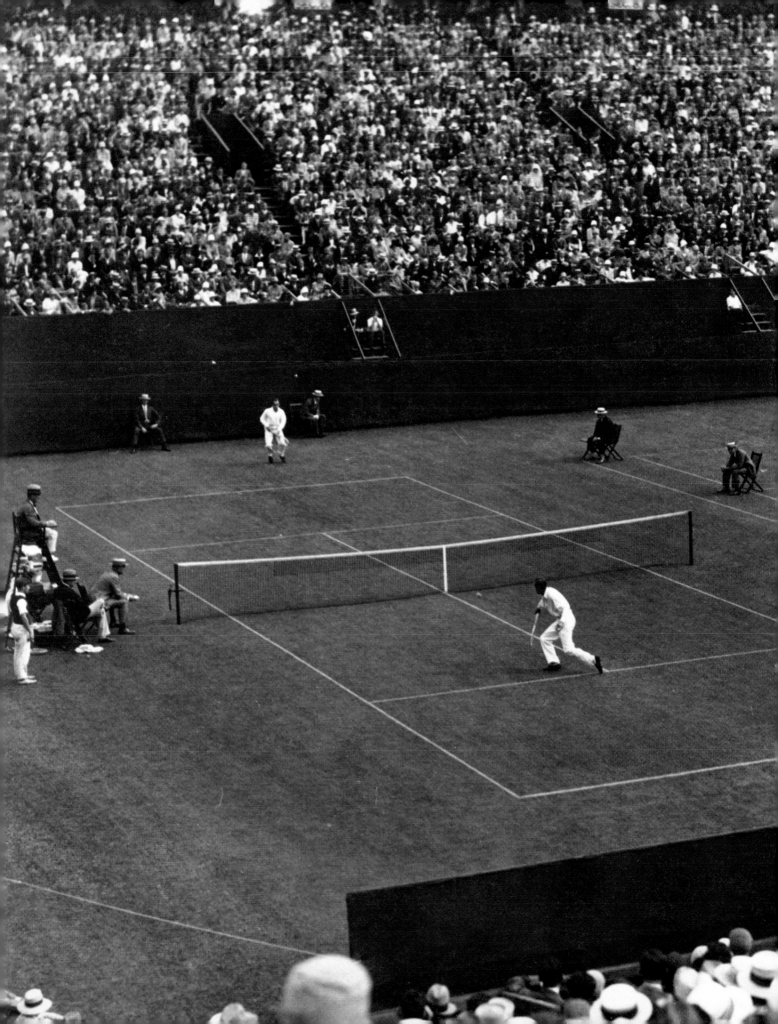

tions. Combining with Frank T. Hunter, Tilden won the doubles championships over the Cochet-Brugnon team at both Wimbledon and Forest Hills, while losing to Lacoste in the singles at the latter tournament. In those days, even for an egotist like Tilden, playing for your country for the cup was considered a higher honor than merely playing for yourself at Wimbledon or Forest Hills. Indeed, the nationalistic overtones of these matches had much to do with exciting tennis interest among nonplayers. They reveled in the fantasy that a country's honor was somehow at stake in the exclusive stadiums where these mysterious people played their mysterious game.

The opening-round pairings pitted Lacoste against Johnston, Tilden against Cochet, with their opponents reversed in the second singles round. In the first match Johnston was pathetic, Lacoste taking him in short, straight sets. Tilden, however, temporarily exorcised the Cochet jinx in four hard sets, giving the United States hope if it could win the doubles. Here USLTA officialdom, despite the desperate situation, decided to teach the arrogant and unpopular Tilden a lesson. They informed him, on the morning of the match, that a player named Dick Williams would be substituted for Frank Hunter as Tilden's partner, despite the fact that that year Tilden-Hunter had proved themselves the world's premier doubles team. Tilden told the men in the blue blazers that he would play with Hunter, one of his few close friends among his fellow competitors —they called themselves "the Smarties"—or he would not play at all. He was informed that he must follow instructions, which was the wrong approach to "Big Bill" Tilden. "Gentlemen," he is said to have said, "I will be playing bridge, and when you have decided to name Mr. Hunter as my partner, come and inform me." With that, he settled back for a day at his second-favorite game.

Periodically through the day, USLTA officials and their emissaries pleaded with Tilden. They were finally told to stop interrupting the bridge game. The audience was in its seats before officialdom conceded their match to the champion and informed Tilden that he could play with Hunter after all. "Fine. I'll dress as soon as we finish this rubber," he told them in his most imperious manner, rather like Sir Francis Drake finishing his game of bowls before taking on the Spanish Armada.

The French Armada, however, did not have everything staked on a single battle. It would be sufficient, after Tilden's hard-fought win over Cochet, simply to extend him as far as they could, wearing him down for Lacoste, who was to play him in the singles next day. It required five sets for Tilden and Hunter to defeat Borotra and Brugnon, and when it was over, Tilden said later, he was "absolutely through . . . I was nervous. My reserves were used up in the bickering."

His only hope the next day against Lacoste was to try for a quick, straight-set victory and he came out firing the big serve. Lacoste, with his book and his brilliant tennis brain, resolved simply to keep everything in play, to run Tilden into the ground. The strategy worked: "The monotonous regularity with which that unsmiling, drab, almost dull man returned the best I could hit . . . often filled me with a wild desire to throw my racket at him," Tilden wrote in his autobiography many years later. He was able to take only one set from the Frenchman, twelve years his junior. It was true, as many witnesses to Tilden's career have testified, that even in defeat he carried himself like a victor, much to everyone's annoyance. This time, however, the crowd at the Germantown Cricket Club took him at his own assessment and when he left the court, they rose in wild ovation—for the first and only time nonplussing Tilden in public. He was used to the galleries' being against him, often worked them around to that mood in order to fire himself up. He did not know what to do with this outburst of affection and raised his arms over his head like a boxer.

Now it was up to the aging and frail Johnston to try to keep the cup in the United States, where it had resided for six years. No one could see how this consistent loser to Tilden could possibly pull out a victory over Cochet, Tilden's most consistent nemesis, yet at the end of two sets they were even. The third set and the early games of the fourth set went easily to Cochet. Johnston, making his last major appearance, rallied, pulling up from 2-5 to 4-5 and

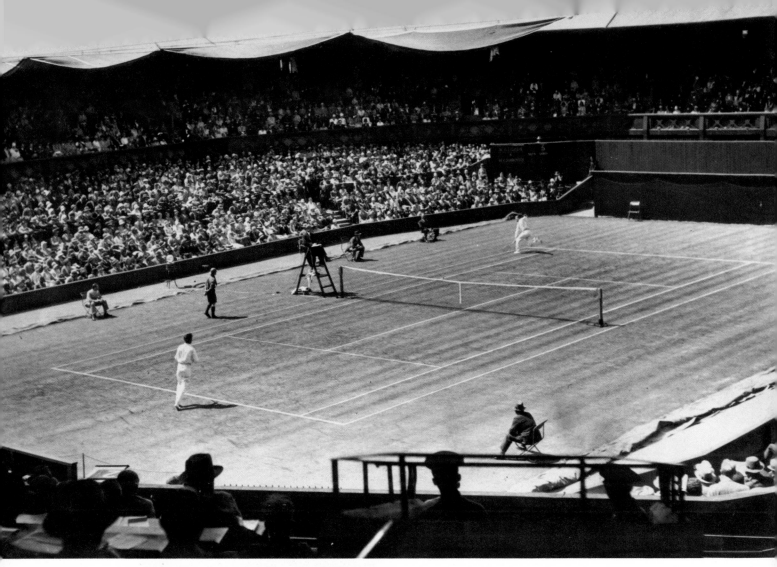

A Yank at Wimbledon. Tilden won
the All England title three times—
most remarkably in 1930, when
he was 37 years old. Centre Court
panorama above was shot in 1928, as he
was beating E. V. Summerson of
Great Britain before losing to Lacoste
in the semis. Left: A practice round.
Right: Tilden and Francis T.
Hunter are seen off on the boat
train after winning the Wimbledon
doubles title in 1927, a feat Tilden
accomplished only this one time.

72

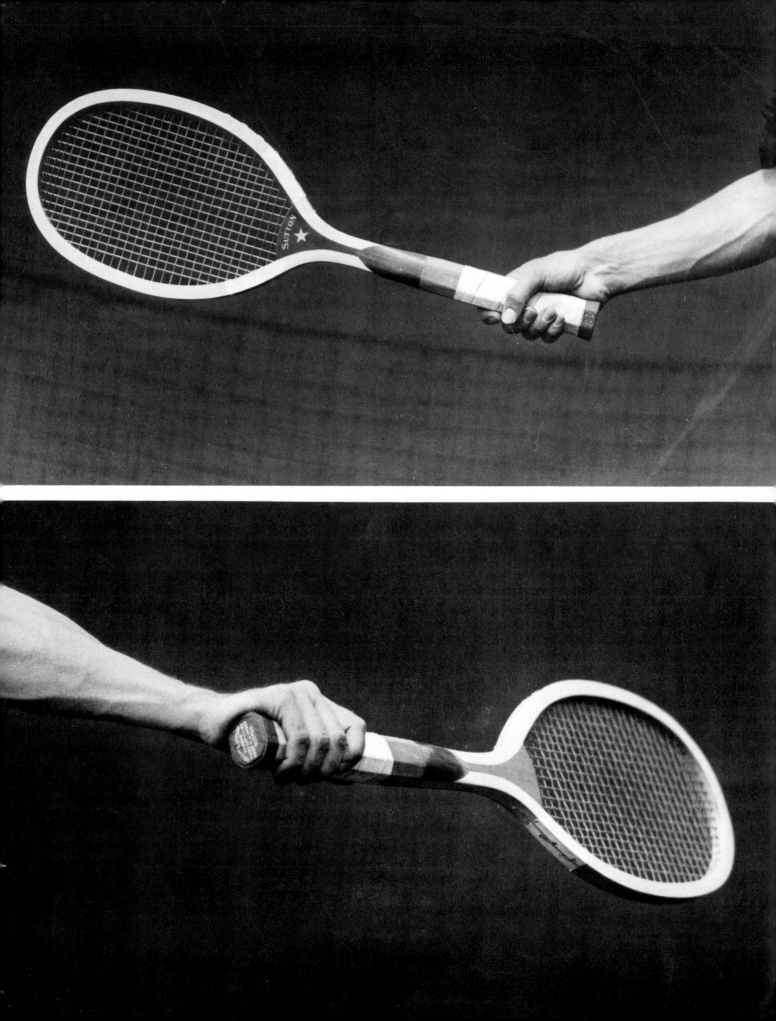

Opposite: Strong right arm of
Richard Norris Williams, twice U.S.
champion and five times a Davis Cupper,
demonstrates forehand grip (top) and
backhand (bottom) for photographer, circa
1920, when such intricacies still
were a revelation to newspaper readers.
Left: Tilden (c) and Frank
Hunter—"the Smarties," as they liked
to style themselves—escort
a group of women internationals to
the courts of the Roehampton
Club for an exhibition.

holding a 30-0 lead in the game that would even the set and very likely even the match. It was a gallant bid, but Johnston was either overanxious or put off by the uproar of the crowd. He finally lost his service, the set, and the match at 6-4, as Tilden sat in the stands next to Lacoste, who was bundled in two sweaters and an overcoat against a nervous chill which even the warm weather and his recent exertions could not penetrate. "God bless you, Little Bill," a woman called out as Johnston's last stand was finally crushed and there was another ovation, this time one washed with tears.

But if the Johnston story in essence ended that day in Philadelphia, the Tilden legend was burnished by defeat. On his return to France Lacoste declared, "Tilden could not be beaten by one player; he was beaten by a team," and the French, who had by this time built a brand new arena, the Stade Roland Garros, mainly to provide a proper setting for the Musketeers, could hardly wait to see them have a go at Tilden on soft red clay.

The USLTA rulers, however, decided that the aging Tilden, supported by Hunter in the doubles and with the undistinguished F. J. Hennessey in the number two singles spot had, in 1928, no real chance of returning the Davis Cup to its native shores. The time was ripe, they fondly believed, for another assault on Tilden. All through the glory years he had listed his occupation as "newspaperman" and, indeed, before becoming a champion he had written on both sports and the theater for the Philadelphia *Ledger*. Ever since, he had filed for sundry syndicates whenever he was engaged in a major championship and he was not the only alleged amateur who picked up some spare change by so doing. The LTA did not much care for the practice, but until now it had chosen to look the other way. This year, however, in a spasm of purity, it decided to suspend Tilden for six months because of the articles he had written from Wimbledon. He was not required for the Inter-Zone finals against Italy, but the French, with tickets to the challenge round at Roland Garros sold out, were beside themselves when it appeared that Tilden would not be permitted to play there. He thoroughly enjoyed his role as international martyr to hypocritical amateurism and

must have enjoyed a particular thrill of satisfaction when the American ambassador in Paris, Myron T. Herrick, acting under pressure from President Coolidge himself, intervened in the affair and worked out a compromise that postponed the suspension until Forest Hills. His excellency made the announcement of the deal at a lunch just before the challenge round was to begin. Tilden rushed out to practice and was, according to reports, so hysterical that he could hit nothing. And he had to face Lacoste—now four consecutive times a victor over him—in the first round. Worse, he would be facing him on clay, extraordinarily suitable to the Frenchman's game and before a home crowd.

Lacoste won the first set easily, 6-1. Then, suddenly, Tilden abandoned his customary big game and started chopping the ball back at Lacoste with a maddening variety of spins and cuts, utterly bewildering the Frenchman and taking the match in five sets. In the locker room afterward, Lacoste spoke to the press: "Two years ago I knew at last how to beat him. Now, on my own court, he beats me. I never knew how the ball would come off the racket, he concealed it so. I had to wait to see how much it was spinning, and sometimes it didn't spin at all. Is he not the greatest player of them all?"

It was the only match Tilden and the Americans won and, indeed, it was 1933 before France gave up the Davis Cup—to a team from Great Britain headed by Fred Perry and H. W. "Bunny" Austin. In the intervening years Tilden was, until he turned pro in 1931, always in the American side and, with Lacoste retired, generally able to defeat Borotra, but never Cochet. Nevertheless, he was by no means washed up. In 1929, when Cochet did not defend his Forest Hills title, Tilden won it for the last time, defeating his pal Hunter in the finals.

Then at Wimbledon in 1930 Wilmer Allison, a fine young American player, defeated Cochet in the quarterfinals, and Tilden, now thirty-seven, took Borotra in the semifinals and downed Allison in the anticlimactic finals. It was a magnificent accomplishment for a player of his age, and he provided an interesting response to René Lacoste, who in *Lacoste on Tennis*, two years before, had stated that

75

it would be interesting to compare the style of the 1920 Wimbledon winner with that of the 1930 winner, implying that the intervening decade would have worked considerable change on the style of the champion. Maybe it did. Certainly the 1930 champion was slower, less vigorous, somewhat cannier in his methods of attack. But the name was the same—Tilden, William Tatem Tilden II.

And he had one more contribution to make to the game. As early as 1926 he had been approached by the legendary C. C. "Cash and Carry" Pyle, the sports promoter, with a $50,000 offer to turn pro, money that neither the hard-hitting and very promising Vinnie Richards nor the great Suzanne Lenglen had been able to resist. "Mr. Tilden, I think you're a damned fool," Pyle had said when Tilden finally turned him down, and Tilden replied, "Mr. Pyle, I think you are probably right." Now, however, he had his last chance to turn his gift to profit and he signed with MGM to make some movies. He was madly stage-struck, having even appeared as Dracula in a New York production. His movie career never amounted to much—he was a very bad actor off the tennis court—but he did launch a profitable pro tour pitted against the Czech champion, Karel Kozeluh, and Richards, both of whom he was able more or less regularly to defeat.

A couple of years later Cochet and Ellsworth Vines, a hard hitter whom many had expected to reach Tildenesque heights, joined the tour. Now Tilden found he could handle Cochet and he generally fought Vines, eighteen years his junior, on even terms, as a little later he would the great Fred Perry, his successor as the dominant figure in world amateur tennis. In fact, Tilden later toured with the much younger Don Budge and with Bobby Riggs, playing solid tennis when he was in his fifties. There was even a fabled occasion, during World War II, when Gardner Mulloy arranged some exhibition matches for the benefit of the Navy and asked Tilden to play a warm-up match before Mulloy took on Ted Schroeder, the Forest Hills champion. Tilden said he would play only if given a shot at Schroeder. Mulloy at first demurred, unwilling to be a party to the old gentleman's humiliation, but finally succumbed. Tilden

snappily defeated Schroeder 6-2, 6-2. He was capable of that almost until the day he died—short bursts of absolutely superlative tennis against anyone.

More important, however, his presence in professional ranks gave that struggling game a respectability it might otherwise not have had in the thirties and forties. Because he had made the jump, others could follow and by so doing they kept a steady pressure on the amateur game to reform, to open itself to professionalism. In the thirties and forties I can remember men of my father's age wondering why in the world, if open golf tournaments were so successful, open tennis tournaments could not be equally so; why the best players in the world were somehow prevented from competing in the world's best tournaments. It may be that Tilden's final victory over the clubmen, the shamans of shamateurism who had sniped away at him all during the years when he was their meal ticket, the star who sold admissions at their box offices, came during the years when his example served to lure their new attractions away from them prematurely, when wandering the world he and his various troupes brought exemplary, world-class tennis to places which otherwise would never have had the chance to see it, extending interest in the game beyond the boundaries of the country-club lawns.

True to form, they turned their back on him when he entered upon his time of troubles in the late forties. He appeared at Forest Hills after serving his jail terms and was snubbed unmercifully. Some literally turned their backs on him when he approached. His name was purged from the alumni files at Penn, his pictures taken down from the walls at his home club, the Germantown Cricket Club. You can find his picture—an old wire-service snap—mixed indiscriminately among those of the other champions (none of whom are legends in quite the Tilden manner) in the men's locker room at Forest Hills. But that's it. There is today no other monument of any sort, anywhere in the small official world of tennis, to the man who made the great world conscious of the game—its beauty, its glory. For a sport that sets such store by tradition it is a very odd omission. Or is it, perhaps, all too characteristic of it?

the thirties and forties

In 1930, the year of Tilden's last victory at Wimbledon, a youth not quite nineteen won the prestigious Pacific Southwest tournament in his native Los Angeles so impressively that the veteran Richard N. Williams declared him to be the best thing to happen to American tennis in a decade. Within a year most of the experts were busy agreeing with the prescient Williams, predicting that the lad would dominate the new decade much as Tilden had the previous one. He might not win all his tournaments, but he would be the man to beat in any tournament he entered.

The player's name was H. Ellsworth Vines, familiarly known as "Hank," "Skinny," and "Elly." He had learned his game on the public courts of Pasadena and he was a basketball player at the University of Southern California, as well as a tennis star. As tall as he was thin, his sober manner on court was saved from dourness by a quick-breaking grin and an engaging, shambling gait. At the end of that first year in big-time tennis he was ranked tenth in the nation. A year later he was number one and, despite his easy, drawling personal style, a figure who struck terror in the hearts of his opponents. There had been hard hitters in the game before—McLoughlin, Tilden (when he wanted to be), such perennial challengers as Francis X. Shields and Wilmer Allison. But none had quite the weapons—or enjoyed quite the success—that Ellsworth Vines achieved early in the new decade.

His was not quite "the Big Game" of the following decade. As a rule, he did not follow his crashing serve to the net, probably because his volleying was insecure, possibly because, when he was on his game, there was no need to. If his 128-mph serve did not instantly annihilate an opponent, his incredibly powerful groundstrokes could force the man into difficulty almost as effectively as a volley could. In 1931 he won the U.S. clay-courts championship, then swept through the eastern grass-courts tour preliminary to Forest Hills, his chief competition coming from the veteran chip-and-chop artist—and fellow Californian—the left-handed John Doeg. He was put out in the semifinals, however, by George Lott, another "small game" exponent, in four hard-fought sets.

Now Vines was ready for his greatest year. He lost the Queen's Club tournament, the traditional warm-up for Wimbledon, to Harry Hopman, later to be the nonplaying captain of Australia's Davis Cup team and architect of its dominance in that competition in the years immediately after World War II. Wimbledon, however, was a different story. Vines lost only six games in winning his quarterfinal and semifinal matches (the latter against another comer, "Gentleman Jack" Crawford of Australia, who sipped tea at the changeovers and was known for his impeccable dress and sportsmanship). The final was against H. W. "Bunny" Austin, a vital component in the team that regained the Davis Cup for Britain in 1933 and held it until 1936, probably the finest player never to win a major championship, and indubitably the first to wear shorts at Wimbledon. The result: a straight-set victory for Vines in forty minutes.

It was, said Austin later, "like encountering a 150-mile-an-hour hurricane. I was being totally flattened. I simply could not see Vines' service nor could I see his returns to my service." Down 5-0 and 40-love in the final game of the third set, Austin waited for Vines to serve, "watching for his smooth, rhythmic, powerful swing. I waited. I did not move. I saw nothing, only a puff of dust on my service court and then the sound of a ball hitting the stop-netting behind me." It was the last of Vines' thirty service aces in that short match, and to this day Austin claims he does not know if the ball bounced to his left or right on its way past him. What everyone remembers was Vines rushing to put his arms about Austin, trying to console him after the most humiliating finals defeat—at least until Jimmy Connors took Ken Rosewall similarly in 1974—in modern Wimbledon history.

It may have been the young Californian's finest hour, though he did well enough against the French when he lost to Borotra and seemed on the way to defeat by Cochet before pulling out the match 4-6, 0-6, 7-5, 8-6, 6-4, in the unsuccessful American challenge for the Davis Cup that year. It was the Frenchman's first cup-competition loss since 1927 and he entered at Forest Hills determined to demonstrate his mastery of Vines. They met in the finals,

Opening pages: A century of rackets.
Far l: "Harvard" model of 1870s.
Third from l: Slazenger's "Doherty" model
of 1880s. Three flattops in center were
standard for almost fifty years. Jack
Crawford won at Wimbledon as late
as 1933 with a racket that looked like
this. Third from r: Premature
steel-shafted racket of 1920s. No one
could figure out how to marry this frame
with gut string, and metal stringing
was unresponsive to a delicate
touch. Next to it is laminated-wood
racket — designed to cope with
new, high-compression balls — that came
on in 1930s and remains essentially
unchanged. Far r: Commercially
most successful of all metal rackets —
Wilson T-2000, sole preference
author shares with Jimmy Connors.

This page: Ellsworth Vines, in
distinctive white cap,
demonstrates the "lightning forehand"
he combined with a thunderous
serve to produce one of
the more punishing attacks
the game has ever seen.

but again Vines was the victor, this time in straight sets. Young and strong, there seemed no reason why he should not reign for years to come.

And yet, almost as quickly as he arrived, he departed. He joined an American team touring Australia in the winter of 1932–33 (taking his new bride along for a honeymoon) and won only one minor event, losing in the fourth round of the national championships. Nevertheless, Tilden, now managing the pro tour as well as starring in it, made him a tempting offer and for merely entertaining it Vines' amateur standing was closely scrutinized by the USLTA, continuing its war with Tilden by other means. Vines was cleared of any wrongdoing, but was humiliatingly forced by the captain of the U.S. Davis Cup team to show him a letter from Tilden before being allowed to play. The letter was a perfectly innocent good-luck wish.

Whether this had an effect on Vines' tennis that summer, no one knows, but he could not defend his Wimbledon title successfully. He again defeated Cochet (in the semis) and then faced Jack Crawford in a final that many regard as one of the three or four greatest in the history of the championship. Gentleman Jack was a classicist, four years older than Vines, shorter and heavier, and anything but a power player. Indeed, with his old-fashioned square-top racket and the long-sleeved cricket shirt he affected (he would roll up the sleeve on his racket arm when the going became tense), he inevitably reminded spectators of a far earlier tennis age, just as the youthful Vines, so much more dependent on sheer power than any other major player, suggested the wave of the future. Thus, even as the players stepped out on to Centre Court, the match shaped up as a contest between the new order and the old.

It opened with Vines firing his big guns—the serve and the forehand that had devastated Austin in 1932—and he took the first set comfortably, 6-4. Crawford had the advantage of first serve in the next set and now switched tactics. Instead of trying to keep the ball constantly on Vines' relatively weak backhand, he began mixing his attack, offering the Californian high-bouncing shots to his forehand. It looked suicidal, but Vines had been having some trouble with his forehand during the tournament and he had difficulty finding the groove on these shots which he was forced to take higher than was his wont. When after three or four such rallies he found it, Crawford returned to the attack on Vines' backhand. He finally took the set at 11-9, and Vines, tiring, his first serves not going in as often as he would have wished, gave Crawford the third set 6-2. Then it was Crawford's turn to surrender a set without much fight, also by 6-2. The final set was decided in the tenth game, Vines serving with the score at 4-5, neither player having lost his serve. Vines was now following serve to net and Crawford took the first point with a lob that just cleared the American's racket. The Australian took the next with a fine shot to Vines' backhand which he could not handle. His third point came on what is commonly regarded as the shot of the match: a backhand half-volley return of service that sizzled cross-court, just out of the charging Vines' reach. Match point. Vines faulted the first serve, hit a weak second serve which Crawford took on the forehand, hitting a ball that Vines could only net. In the stands, Mrs. Crawford fainted from the strain.

She quickly recovered, but Vines did not. In the Inter-Zone Davis Cup matches against Britain a little later in the year, Austin defeated Vines almost as easily as he had been beaten by him at Wimbledon the year before. Then the American sprained his ankle in the fourth set of his match against the man who would replace him as the world's premier tennis player, Fred Perry. He gamely continued the close, hard-fought match, but down 6-7 in the fifth set, with two match points against him, Vines collapsed and had to concede the rubber. Austin and Perry, of course, went on to finally end the six-year French dominance of Cup play, defeating the aging Musketeers (*sans* Lacoste) 3-2 shortly thereafter. A little after *that* Vines was defeated in the fourth round of the U.S. tournament by Bryan M. "Bitsy" Grant, after which he turned pro before his reputation could be further tarnished. On long tours with the Tilden troupe he seemed to regain something of his old form, defeating Tilden in one series, tying, then beating Perry in a couple of long tours after the great Englishman began play-

Below: H. W. ``Bunny'' Austin was a Davis Cupper for nine years, playing singles with teammate Fred Perry in glory years of British supremacy, 1933-36. He also introduced shorts as acceptable court costume. Here he tops Allison of U.S. in 1935. Left: Bryan M. ``Bitsy'' Grant takes measure of Australia's Adrian Quist — for years a phenomenal doubles player with John Bromwich — at Forest Hills in 1938. Following pages: **Tennis,** oil, William Glackens, 1909.

ing for pay, then succumbing at last to Don Budge when he turned pro. Even then, he did not vanish from the sports pages, for he took up golf and was a steady money winner on the pro tour in the 1940s.

Still, his was a curious case. There are veteran tennis experts who still believe that Vines, during that period of less than two years when he was virtually unbeatable, may have played the greatest tennis in the history of the game, and notwithstanding the suddenness of his descent, he regularly appears on all-time ten-best lists.

What happened to him? Why couldn't he sustain himself for a longer period in tournament competition? One can only speculate, but it appears that he was truly a man ahead of his time, perhaps ahead of himself. That is to say, he had the physical equipment and the intelligence to understand that the power game was the game of the future, but did not entirely understand all that it required of a man to play it consistently over longer periods of time. For example, his potent forehand was of the so-called "western" variety, meaning that it lacked the topspin which is required to control its force. When Vines was off, he simply had no equipment to bring forehand under control and keep it within the baseline. Similarly, that big serve required not just occasional forays to the net, but the consistent ability to follow it with killing volleys. Very often all he was doing was giving opponents (like Crawford on that last shot at Wimbledon) some of his own power to throw back at him, especially if they were quick enough to take his shots on the rise.

Obviously, these were matters with which he successfully came to grips in the course of his long pro tours, at roughly the same time that Don Budge was carefully putting together the elements of a similar style in the amateur ranks. It is also worth pointing out that after he had got himself together he was not only a consistent winner on the touring circuit, but the coach of the player whose name became synonymous with the Big Game, the first man to play tennis in the manner that has become standard—even rather boringly so—in modern tennis, Jack Kramer.

It seems likely that what happened to Vines was that he suffered severe confusion and a sudden, profound loss of confidence once his opponents ceased to be awed by his terrible swift speed, began analyzing the rest of his game and finding its weaknesses. It also seems likely that he could have staged a comeback as an amateur if he had been able to withdraw from competition for a while and work with a first-class coach of the sort world-class players nowadays routinely consult when their games go sour. He was not able to do that, and it is doubtful in those days that he could have found a guru capable of helping him, there not being anything like the number of superconsultants available then as there is now. Indeed, it is amazing how many of the great players of this and previous periods were essentially self-taught.

This was true of the man who replaced Vines as the game's dominant figure, Fred Perry, who simultaneously cut short Jack Crawford's brilliant run at a Grand Slam and also announced his own arrival as a figure to contend with at the 1933 Forest Hills championship. Crawford had taken the Australian championship for the third consecutive time that year, defeated Cochet for the French title, and his historic victory over Vines at Wimbledon had given him the third leg on this great achievement. He arrived at Forest Hills tired and over-tennised and in the midst of a heat wave that made sleep nearly impossible for him. Nonetheless, he struggled through to the finals, where Perry, who had been on the scene for some years, and who had teamed with Austin to win Britain's first Davis Cup since 1912, awaited him.

Crawford confessed to Vinnie Richards that his nerves were bothering him and to Richards' practiced eye it was self-evident that the Australian was drawn awfully fine. He said he had a secret nerve tonic—never mind what it was—that he would slip into the iced tea Gentleman Jack habitually sipped at changeovers, and Crawford gladly accepted the offer. The tonic was nothing more than a stiff shot of bourbon and it seemed to help for awhile. Tight—in one sense of the word—Crawford lost the first set 6-3, then loosened up to take the next two, very hard-fought, sets

13-11, 6-4. Thereafter, however, he appears to have been tight in the other sense of the word, winning but a single game in the last two sets.

It may be, of course, that Richards' tonic had nothing to do with the case, that Perry, who was always a superbly conditioned athlete, simply had too much stamina for Crawford on that steamy day. In any event, it was the first major victory for a great and extremely interesting player.

Fred Perry was the first distinguished British player who was not a public-school product. His father was a Labor M.P., and Perry himself had been a table-tennis champion before taking up lawn tennis. Indeed, it is said his interest in the game was aroused because he asked his father who owned the large number of splendid automobiles he had noticed parked around some courts near his home. Told that they belonged to the tennis players, Perry is said to have replied, "Well, if they can have cars like that, that's for me." Apocryphal or not, the story neatly fits the character he displayed on the center courts of the world. He was an ambitious young man when he first joined a team of English players touring the United States grass-court circuit in 1930. There, he later recalled, he picked up the American attitude toward the game, the attitude "of never wanting to be second." He added: "When I played I went out there to come in first, and I think a lot of English people didn't understand or realize that in those days."

Certainly, at first, they did not understand what he was trying to do with his game. He used the continental grip, which is not unlike the grip most of us employ when wielding a hammer, and it is not a grip one changes when switching from forehand to backhand. Generally speaking, it requires a player to sacrifice power for speed, and it is basically a scrambler's grip, not usually associated with offensive-minded players. Perry, however, was not only quick of foot, but had extraordinary hand-eye coordination. This, coupled with his early table-tennis training, enabled him to get to the ball more quickly than most, and to impart great power to his forehand in particular, with a forceful wrist snap. When a veteran tournament official

and manufacturer of tennis equipment named A. R. "Pops" Summers proposed that Perry employ his quickness to get to the ball early, thus taking it on the rise and using his naturally wristy stroke to snap the ball back at opponents with unexpected force, he completed the process of shaping a great tennis style. Or almost did, for it took Perry the better part of a season to control his rebuilt game, and he had to withstand considerable protest from members of his home club who objected to having their games interrupted by the spray of wildly hit balls from Perry's practice court. He has, in fact, said that he never totally mastered the self-imposed intricacies of his style, that even late in his career, when he was touring pro, he suffered long days when he simply could not hit the ball confidently. Be that as it may, until he turned pro in 1937, Fred Perry was the unchallenged master of world-class tennis.

In 1934 he and Crawford met once again in the finals of a major championship—Wimbledon. At Forest Hills the previous summer Perry had come out attacking. Now he decided to play a waiting game, extending rallies in the opening set in an attempt to wear some of the edge off Crawford's game. This he apparently accomplished to his satisfaction while taking the first set 6-3. In the second, Perry attacked more violently and won it without the loss of a game. Crawford, a fine competitor, extended him in the third set, but went down 7-5, and Wimbledon had its first native champion since Arthur Gore's victory in 1909.

Perry repeated as Wimbledon champion the next two years, and those wins remain an unprecedented feat in modern tennis history. Budge, Laver, Hoad, Newcombe won the title twice in a row, but none of them matched Perry's three-in-a-row performance. Nor has an Englishman since won Wimbledon.

There cannot have been a more popular victory than Perry's first at the All England Club. The year before, when the English had wrested the Davis Cup from France, largely through Perry's efforts, most of the nation had been glued to its radios, listening to the broadcasts from the Stade Roland Garros across the channel. Everyone knew that Perry had fainted after winning his first singles against

Now and Future King: Fred Perry, having helped Britain gain the Davis Cup for the first time since 1912, and having spoiled Jack Crawford's bid for a Grand Slam by winning at Forest Hills, defeats Johnny Van Ryn in semis at Pacific Southwest in 1933. He went on to win the tournament — and twice defend his title.

Cochet, knew that he had been held out of the doubles and forbidden to practice in order to conserve his strength for what everyone knew would be the deciding match, against Andre Merlin, nineteen years old and, as his name implied, a wizard. Everyone knew, too, that in those concluding five sets Perry had played himself right off his feet, that when the cup officially changed hands on court he was prostrate in the locker room, unable to attend the ceremonies.

Thus he was already an heroic figure to the home crowds when he won his national title the next year, so much so that although the king had not been present to see the victory, he specifically requested that Perry appear the next day at Centre Court and be presented to His Majesty, who apologized for missing the great event. What His Majesty did not know was that Perry had been out partying all night after his win, that he was still in white tie and tails and quite unshaven when the call came ordering him to report back to the Centre Court stadium for the royal presentation. His father had to meet him there with a proper suit, and he managed to get a shave in the locker room before being taken out to enjoy his triumphal moment.

He has always spoken with a degree of awe of the monarch's apology for missing his famous victory over Crawford, but there was always a slightly parodistical edge to Perry's portrayal of the proper Englishman in public. For example, he took to sucking a pipe around the world's tennis clubs, but no one ever saw it lit and many believed that there was rarely even any tobacco in its bowl. He generally ordered that most pukka of drinks, a gin and tonic, but most people claimed there was never any gin in the glass. On court he never disputed a linesman's call, but he did like to wag a finger at the offending official and say something like "naughty boy" when he erred—very Mr. Chips. And, of course, he is famous for having turned down a royalty that might have amounted to a million pounds or so when he refused an offer to endorse Daks slacks in order to retain his amateur status and help England defend the Davis Cup one last time in 1936. The socialist's boy was showing the swells that he could not only beat them at their own game, but equal them in the gentlemanly graces. Yet

shortly after turning professional, he also became an American citizen, saying goodbye to all that. He has become one of the tennis world's most successful businessmen, and his tennis shirts, with their laurel wreath emblem, rival Lacoste's alligator-emblazoned apparel in popularity. Meantime, he added two more American titles, the French, and the Australian to his record, and never lost a Davis Cup match.

Along the way, Perry took time to help a tall, red-haired California teen-ager with his footwork. A lot of other people, recognizing a great natural talent, did the same. Sidney Wood, the American who won Wimbledon in 1931, helped straighten out some serious problems the youth was having with his forehand grip; the coach at his local club, a man named Tom Stow, braced his net game after he had lost a disappointing series of matches to small baseline retrievers; his brother, Lloyd, worked constantly with him to make him, arguably, the greatest player in the history of the game.

The player's name, of course, was J. Donald Budge, hero of the United States quest for return of the Davis Cup, first of the two men ever to win the Grand Slam, and in everyone's view one of the game's great sportsmen, a player of charm and character and, oddly, a youth who considered tennis an unworthy, even sissified, game until he was nagged into giving it a serious try when he was fifteen—just seven years before he won his first Wimbledon. His father was a Scotsman who had played soccer for the Glasgow Rangers and, as a kid, Budge had thought that a suitable game, though it was difficult to find much competition around Oakland, California, where he grew up. Baseball was considered a worthy alternative and he played a lot of that with, he later liked to say, excellent effect on his famous backhand, since for some reason he had always batted left-handed, making it all the easier for him to approach a tennis ball from the wrong side and still hit out freely.

It was his older brother, Lloyd, who was the family tennis nut and it was he who goaded his fifteen-year-old sibling into taking up the game in his midteens.

Scenes from a tennis life.
Left: Perry and Crawford pose amiably — although Fred robbed Jack of his Grand Slam by taking Forest Hills singles from him in 1933. Below: Perry vs. Austin for British Hard Court (clay) championship at Bournemouth the same year. Perry won — as he also did against Wilmer Allison defending U.S. title in '34 (r). Far r: A balletic overhead at Wimbledon in 1936.

The 1930 California State boys' championship was coming up, and Lloyd suggested that Donald, who had shown some natural gift for tennis when he was around ten, might like to practice briefly, enter, and see how he could do. It was the kind of silly challenge that appeals to an adolescent's sense of bravado; it would be fun to see if he could take a few matches against youngsters who, in California in those days (and these), would have spent the summer pointing toward the tournament. Budge worked away with a battered old racket for a week or so, entered, wearing old corduroy pants, and bludgeoned his way to the final. His father bought him some respectable white flannels for that match and Budge won his first trophy—a triumph in its way as remarkable as any he would enjoy on the world stage later.

It was three years before Budge won the next class in his state championships—the junior title—but he did it in style, winning the men's title in the same tournament. Thereafter he sharpened his game on both the eastern circuit and on European tours. By 1936 he was playing

Davis Cup for the United States and that year, too, he reached the semifinals at Wimbledon and the finals at Forest Hills, losing both times to Perry. When the latter turned pro at the end of that season, it was obvious that Budge's time had come. He won the Wimbledon title handily, defeating Gottfried von Cramm, the aristocratic and graceful German player, in late years a perpetual runner-up to Perry and others on the international circuit, and the only player on the scene close to Budge's caliber.

It looked as if Budge and his Davis Cup teammates, who included Bitsy Grant, Frank Parker, and Budge's great friend and expert doubles partner, Gene Mako, would easily win their Inter-Zone match against the Germans, then go on to defeat the Perry-less English team for the cup.

Unfortunately, however, those in charge of the American team found themselves under pressure to play Grant, not Parker, in the number two singles spot. Grant was a tiny, popular player who had been around for awhile, occasionally beating players ranked higher than he was

94

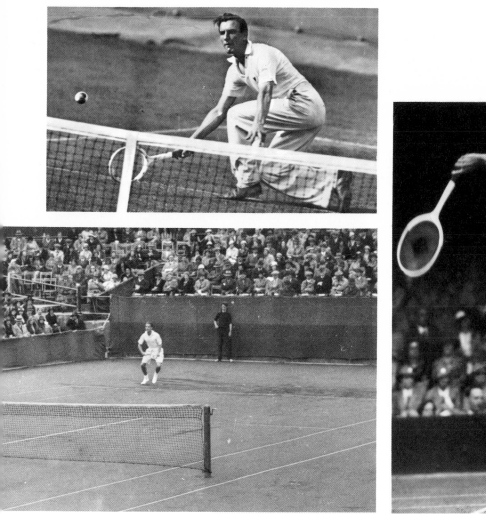

—usually on their off days—and he was not getting any younger. Many thought he should have the honor. They also believed it possible that he was discriminated against because he was a southerner, not therefore a natural member of the Eastern-California axis that ruled the USLTA. So he got the nod and lost his first match to von Cramm while Budge easily stood off Henner Henkel, the German number two. Next day Budge and Mako took the doubles from von Cramm and Henkel, and in the dressing room on the final day of the competition Budge was hopeful that Grant would defeat Henkel, so that his match against von Cramm would be just an exhibition.

Probably the Baron hoped the same thing. Tall, blond, blue-eyed, he seemed the very embodiment of German theories about the racial superiority of the Nordic type. With Hitler still smarting from Germany's disappointing performance at the 1936 Berlin Olympics, he felt enormous pressure to regain national honor here. It was not the sort of pressure he welcomed, since he loathed the Nazis and, indeed, a year later would be arrested by the Gestapo on some trumped-up charge.

Alas, there was to be no escape from the pressure. Grant lost to Henkel in four sets and now von Cramm was forced to delay for a few moments his entrance to Centre Court in order to accept a hortatory phone call from Hitler himself. Despite it, the Baron came on strong. Budge broke him in the ninth game of the first set and had only to hold service to win 6-4. By his own account he served four beauties, every one of which von Cramm returned with perfect placements to break at love. Four games later he broke Budge again to win the set 8-6. The second set also went to von Cramm, 7-5, his beautiful placements preventing Budge from coming to net, his relentless pressure causing Budge's forehand to falter.

Anger, according to Budge, came to his rescue as the third set began. He knew he was playing great tennis and he was convinced that his greatest was better than the German's greatest. Having to win the third set, he varied his tactics, taking von Cramm's serves on the rise and forcing his way to the net, until then territory that had belonged

J. Donald Budge demonstrates
what may be the most
famous backhand in tennis
history. By rolling it,
he turned what had been a
purely defensive weapon into a
potent offensive stroke.
Scene is the Wimbledon
final of 1938, where Budge
successfully defended his
title with a straight-set
victory over perpetual
also-ran, Bunny Austin.

to the German. Budge had one suspenseful moment in the fourth game, when von Cramm again shot back four consecutive winners off Budge's best serves, but the American rallied immediately to take the Baron's serve at love and the momentum of his victory in that set carried him through both the intermission and the next set, which Budge took 6-2.

It was 7:30 when the final set began. Dusk was falling and the already fast court was now becoming slippery with dew. In the fourth game von Cramm broke Budge's serve, two winners on the American's forehand side being decisive. He then held his own serve at love and all sorts of drama erupted.

Bill Tilden was coaching the Germans, not out of any love for them, but as yet another way of tweaking the noses of his old enemies at the USLTA. At this point he stood up, raised his hand with thumb and forefinger forming a circle, as if to say to Henkel and the rest of the German contingent at courtside, "It's in the bag." This drew an instant response from the American cheering section headed by Paul Lukas, the émigré Hungarian romantic actor, Jack Benny, the comedian, and Ed Sullivan, then known only as a newspaper columnist. They came close, it would seem, to engaging Tilden in a most un-Wimbledonian fist fight. Meantime, down on the court, Walter Pate, the nonplaying American captain, tossed Budge a towel and the player tossed him a few encouraging words. There is considerable variance in the sources as to what, exactly, Budge said on this historic occasion, but it was something along the lines of "Don't count us out yet, Cap. I'm not tired and I feel great." It is not important what he said. To have said anything at all optimistic when you are down 4-1 in the deciding set of the political grudge match of the century must be counted an act of great moral fortitude.

Yet Budge was as good as his word. He won his serve at love and was now only two games behind. He noticed at this point that von Cramm was uncommonly eager to get the balls and begin serving. Perhaps he was overanxious, too eager to run out the set, Budge thought. He

guessed that, as so often happens in this circumstance, his opponent might begin hurrying his first serve. If he started missing that, Budge thought, he would cheat up a few steps on the second, catch it on the rise, and rifle it back at the German. That precisely is what he was able to do as he broke von Cramm's serve at 4-3, and held on to his own to even the set. Now von Cramm's greatest weakness, a weakness also said to beset the German military mind—an inability to vary his attack—began to haunt him. He kept pounding away at Budge's formerly vulnerable forehand, now suddenly impregnable. In the thirteenth game Budge broke von Cramm "without . . . any shots of distinction" and had only to hold his serve to run out the match.

They played eighteen points in that concluding game, five of them match points. According to Budge's estimate, five minutes elapsed between the first and the last of these—an eternity on the tennis player's inner clock. It was then, in the gathering gloom, under almost unbearable pressure, that Budge made what many consider to be the greatest single shot of the century. An exchange of groundstrokes had taken both players to the right-hand side of the court, where Budge fired what he considered was a good backhand, von Cramm returned a beautiful cross-court forehand, moving to the net behind it. In an instant, Budge knew that his only hope was a running—indeed, lunging —forehand, that would leave him on his knees, the entire court open to von Cramm's riposte. There was, however, to be no answer to the shot he hit, a deep, thundering drive down the left side, that landed no more than six inches inside the baseline, the same distance inside the sideline. From his inglorious position Budge could not see if it was in or out, but he could see the linesman's hands extended palms downward in the "safe" gesture.

It was over. Von Cramm was awaiting him at the net as Budge scrambled to his feet. They embraced and the Baron said: "Absolutely the finest match I've ever played in my life. I'm happy I could play it against you, whom I like so much." Budge said later he felt close to tears and was quite certain von Cramm was also.

Budge, now teamed with Parker, led the Ameri-

Right: "Tennis at Newport" is an impressionistic view of a social evening at the Casino in 1919, by George Bellows. Below: A collection of antique presses and carrying cases surround an ingenious curiosity —a cork-handled lady's racket of the 1880s. Carved wood was standard from the game's beginning until the 1930s—perhaps because early manufacturers borrowed from cricket-bat tradition.

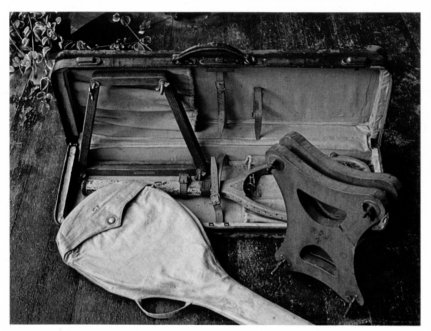

cans to a 4-1 victory over Great Britain in the Davis Cup challenge round, then defeated von Cramm in the Forest Hills finals later in the summer of 1937. But his greatest feat, in the eyes of the USLTA, was resisting a $50,000 offer to turn pro. Had they but noticed, the handwriting was on the wall. The best young players were not waiting, as Tilden had, until their late thirties before capitalizing on their talent, and the gentlemen at 120 Broadway in New York, where the USLTA had its offices, were childishly grateful to Budge for holding off another year—until he was all of twenty-two—before deserting them.

Unwittingly, of course, he did himself a favor in agreeing to remain an amateur and help defend the Davis Cup he had just won. It gave him the opportunity to go for his Grand Slam, which—looking for a new challenge—he quite deliberately set out to accomplish. He arrived in Australia well in advance of the national tournament there, which is played in January, and loafed through the warm-up tournaments, giving the locals a false sense of equality with him and keeping himself fresh for the big one. He took it without the loss of a single set, defeating the fine John Bromwich 6-3, 6-1, 6-2 in the finals. He lost two sets on his way to the French championship, where his greatest thrill seems to have been his encounter with Pablo Casals, the cellist, who came to watch all his matches. Finally he said: "Don, I got so much enjoyment from watching you play that I would like to invite you back to my house tonight to play for you." Which he did, Budge and the other guests sprawled at the master's feet in his studio, a moonlit Paris visible through the window.

Wimbledon was more of the same, with Budge again not losing a set in the entire tournament, where he defeated Bunny Austin in the finals. Forest Hills was a little tougher, since his opponent in the finals was Gene Mako, who knew Budge's game intimately and had also been playing extremely well all season. To tighten the tension it began raining as soon as the semifinal round was finished, and Budge and Mako had to wait a full week before the weather cleared enough for them to play the final. Budge's apprehensions proved false; Mako took only one set. Now,

with the Grand Slam behind him and the Davis Cup safely defended, Budge was free to turn pro and the USLTA Pooh Bahs actually joined him at the press conference to wish him well in his new career.

That, however, was more a tribute to Budge's winning manner than a signal that they were changing heart on the whole pro-amateur question. Indeed, their treatment of the man who helped Budge defend the Davis Cup and succeeded him as Wimbledon and Forest Hills champion was much more typical. It might even be said to have contributed something to his eccentric public style, which has become more familiar to modern tennis buffs than his really quite distinguished playing record. That player's name, of course, is Bobby Riggs.

He had been marked down as a troublemaker right from the start. He was a poor kid who won his first tennis racket shooting marbles, scrambled his way through California junior ranks with no encouragement from the West Coast ruling powers, notably the powerful Perry Jones, who in Riggs' view cared more about a young player's social background and how he dressed than he did about ability. "He liked his young tennis players to be tall, immaculate in white tennis clothes and respectfully polite"—none of which the five-foot seven-inch, endlessly cheeky and chattering Bobby was. Worse, his game was not the serve-and-volley game that had become California's trademark. He was a baseliner, a retriever who could return anything anyone could throw at him. Worse, even as a youngster he was known to enjoy getting a little money down on himself when he played. The upshot was that he got less financial support from Jones and the rest of the USLTA than many a less-gifted player. Indeed, when he won the U.S. junior title the proffered reward to the winner, a tour of the European tournaments, was suddenly, mysteriously withdrawn. When he refused to defend the title because he was eager to enter senior tournaments, Jones withdrew all support from Riggs, forcing him to scratch his own road to recognition in the East. This discrimination even extended to Davis Cup play. Riggs was allowed to practice with Budge and the rest before they left for Eng-

101

One of the great matches of all
time was decisive five-set struggle
between Budge (below r) and Gottfried von Cramm
in Inter-Zone final between U.S. and
Germany at Wimbledon in 1937.
Budge lost first two sets, was down
1-4 in fifth, but rallied brilliantly to
win. Bill Tilden (on sidelines, l,
with von Cramm in 1935) exacerbated national
feelings by serving as coach of
Germans. Bottom: Von Cramm in process
of beating Bitsy Grant in opening
singles match of the series.

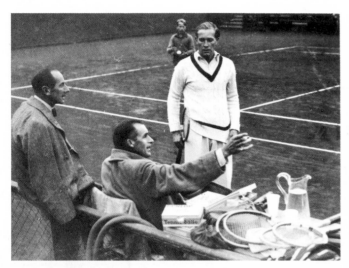

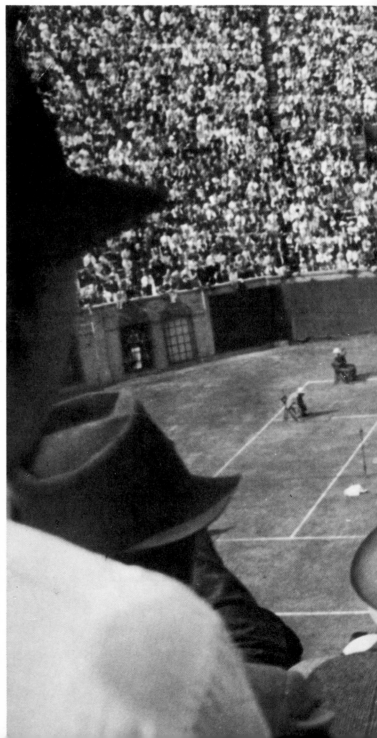

Night of the Big Snow: Riggs (l)
and Kramer play their first professional
match—December 26, 1947—before
sellout Madison Square Garden
crowd which braved a blizzard to
watch guileful little Bobby
score a surprising win over the
powerful Kramer. At tour's end, however,
Kramer had piled up a 69-20 edge.
Note stretchers for fabric
court surface and retaining net
at rear. Opposite: Budge and Riggs with
honors and honorariums, c. 1938.

land and the great encounter with the Germans, but he was not allowed to accompany the team, despite the fact that he could consistently beat everyone on it except Budge.

Long before he won a major title, Riggs was disgusted with amateur tennis, vocal in his criticism of under-the-table payoffs from tournament sponsors (though he says he was able to make a reasonable living from them). By the late thirties he was frankly playing to amass enough important championships to drive up his price for turning professional. In 1938, he contributed what turned out to be the margin of America's victory over Australia in the Davis Cup challenge round by defeating Adrian Quist.

The next year, seeded number one at Wimbledon, he bet about $500 on himself at three to one to win the men's singles, instructing the bookmaker to let his winnings ride (at six to one) in the men's doubles and, if he won that, to put the whole bundle on him and Alice Marble to win the mixed doubles at twelve to one. Miraculously, he did it all, winning $108,000 on the tournament, though he left his pile in an English bank, expecting to collect the next year. Instead, he had to wait six years—until a little inconvenience called World War II was over—before picking up his winnings.

Meantime, he won his first Forest Hills crown, suffered a setback when he and Frank Parker lost the Davis Cup challenge round to Australia, and worst of all failed to repeat his Forest Hills victory, which meant postponing his professional debut until he could re-win the title, which he did in 1941 by beating Frank Kovacs, another, even more comical, psych artist, who immediately joined Riggs in the pro ranks.

As was so often the case in his career, Riggs' timing was bad. He opened his pro tour just nineteen days after Pearl Harbor, and it was six years before he could cash in on his reputation—engaging and soundly defeating Don Budge on a long cross-country tour in 1947. Even then, Budge was the idol, Riggs a pesky villain in the drama—the very roles in which the USLTA had long ago cast them. Indeed, Riggs was still playing the part almost a quarter of a century later, when he emerged from years of exile (in

which he supported himself largely by making hustler's bets on himself at golf, tennis, bridge, or any other sporting event which gave him a sporting chance) to make his infamous challenges to Margaret Court and Billie Jean King.

One doesn't want to make too much of his case and his career; Bobby Riggs is not quite a tragic figure. Yet his history is exemplary in some ways. Interest in the game had expanded steadily in the decades between the wars, distinguished players were coming up out of every class in almost every country. Room had to be made within the amateur game not only for a variety of playing styles, but a variety of life-styles as well. It was cruel to individuals and shortsighted for the game as a whole to try to impose on it the manners and morals of a narrow—and narrow-minded—ruling class, especially when these standards could only be maintained through resort to hypocrisy. Better to have encouraged players like Riggs, instead of driving them into rebelliousness, better to have opened up the little world of tennis than double the guards at the entrance. The life was being choked out of the game while the game was shutting itself off from the life most people led. The war, which effectively halted expansion of the game for a few years, should have provided the sport's rulers with an opportunity to rethink their basic premises. Instead, they emerged from it into the democratically bustling, economically expanding postwar world fundamentally resistant to change. Riggs and the other hustlers and promoters who had passed into their ken were eccentrics, oddballs, people to be "handled." They could not possibly be the wave of the future. The idea was too preposterous to contemplate.

105

assault on tradition

They played tennis at Wimbledon during the war. The clubhouse and some of the facilities under the grandstand were used as dormitories for soldiers, as canteens and aid stations, but the famous grass was weeded by volunteers in moments between more pressing duties and servicemen were welcome to play—even on Centre Court—when they had an hour to spare. At the first possible opportunity after hostilities ended, which turned out to be in the summer of 1946, there was a tournament, though with rationing still in effect the club's liquor allotment consisted of a single bottle per month.

Nor were the foreign delegations of the size they had been and shortly would be again. There were, for example, just two Aussies and two Yanks in the draw, the title eventually going to Yvon Petra of France only a little more than a year removed from a prisoner-of-war camp and well liked by the crowds for his colorful ways, which included donning a jockey's cap when the going got tough.

The United States representatives—and winners of the doubles title—were Tom Brown and Jack Kramer, the latter one of the key figures in tennis history. He was put out of this tournament early on by the great Jaroslav Drobny of Czechoslovakia, principally because of a severe case of blisters on his racket hand.

Kramer had been noted as a comer before the war, winning the national junior title as early as 1935 and becoming at seventeen the youngest American ever to represent his country in a Davis Cup challenge round. (He and Joseph Hunt, another promising youth, who was killed in the war, lost the doubles match to Adrian Quist and John Bromwich.) He had, however, passed the war in the Coast Guard and had, despite many travels, found precious few tennis courts on which to keep his game sharp. Mustered out, and determined to play in the first postwar Wimbledon—at twenty-five he obviously realized that he had only a few years left in which to make his mark as a player—he overpracticed with new rackets, the grips of which were wrapped in a way he was unused to, and destroyed his hand. He had to default at Queens, traditional curtain raiser to Wimbledon, and he had to play wearing a woman's glove with the fingers cut off. During the match against Drobny (one set of which went to 18-16), a Dutch doctor who was also playing in the tournament came out at the changeovers and bandaged and rebandaged the damaged digits. In the end, not unpredictably, Kramer lost to the Czech, who himself did not survive the semifinals.

But it was in some ways the match of Kramer's career. Despite straitened circumstances Wimbledon was still Wimbledon. Kramer's tennis shirt was nothing fancier than a Coast Guard-issue T-shirt, and when he served in Centre Court, he looked into the twisted wreckage where a Nazi bomb had left its mark on the stands. Even so, the grass was the best he had ever seen and he learned more losing to Drobny than he might have winning from him. As he put it to journalist Gwen Robyns, "This game at Wimbledon proved to be a source of strength because tennis is a game of feel, and when you wear a glove on your hand and you have tape all over your fingers you lose a lot of your feel. But almost being able to beat Drobny, who was a damn tough tennis player, was fine. If in the future anything got rough on me out there I used to say to myself it can't ever be as tough as playing Drobny. It provided me with a mental crutch."

That same summer Kramer won at Forest Hills, beating his Wimbledon travelling companion, Tom Brown, in the finals. That winter, along with Ted Schroeder and Gardner Mulloy, he made the long journey to Australia to reclaim the Davis Cup from the bank vault where it had been stored since the Aussies made off with it in 1939. They swept the series, Kramer beating Dinny Pails and Bromwich in his singles matches and teaming with Schroeder to defeat the distinguished and veteran team of Bromwich and Adrian Quist in the doubles. The next season it was common knowledge that if Kramer won at Wimbledon, defended his Forest Hills title successfully, and participated victoriously in the defense of the Davis Cup he would turn professional. He did not feel, having lost so many competitive years during the war, that he had any time to waste before cashing in on his extraordinary talent.

Characteristically, he fulfilled his program pre-

Opening pages: Leonine Pancho
Gonzales has been playing
top-flight tennis since
the late forties, still is
capable of a few phenomenal sets
when his game is on — or
his opponent's is off.
Below: Jack Kramer in action
against Australia's Dinny
Pails en route to his
only Wimbledon championship in
1947. His "Big Game" blasted
traditional baseliners off court.

109

Mingled Lives: Ted Schroeder (l), Davis Cup teammate and longtime doubles partner of Kramer, won 1949 Wimbledon by beating Jaroslav Drobny, self-exiled Czech ace (shown in losing final, r), who had given 1946 Kramer (below) a tennis lesson in fiercely fought early-round Wimbledon match. Far right: Young Kramer changing to spiked shoes.

cisely. As he had the year before, he took along good American steaks in order to add protein to the austerity diet available in England, and even shared the last of them with Tom Brown, his opponent in the Wimbledon final, just before beating him in straight sets.

Frank Parker, the clever baseliner from Milwaukee, was his opponent in the finals at Forest Hills later in the summer, and indeed took the first two sets from Kramer before bowing. Again characteristically, Kramer predicted accurately that he would almost certainly meet Parker if not in the finals of the U.S. championship, then somewhere along the way, and reasoned that since the older, smaller man's backhand was his strongest stroke he, Kramer, would have to hit his forehand cross-court strokes perfectly in order to keep the ball as much as possible to Parker's forehand. Unhappy with this stroke at Wimbledon, he took a plane from London directly to Chicago in order to receive special coaching on the errant shot for a few days. It proved to be a decisive factor in the match.

That was the thing about Kramer. He was a smart player, smarter than most of the fans of the moment realized. They were under the impression that "the Big Game," with which his name will be forever associated, was a dummy's game. Blam—a booming serve—slam—a slashing volley at the net—end of point. To many traditionalists it was all a blur and entirely lacking in the subtlety and delicious suspense that long rallies between baseliners could produce. Of course, players had been coming to net with some regularity for over a quarter of a century. But after virtually every shot? That was not an altogether delightful innovation. It seemed to place a premium on brute strength. Was that the way it was going to be in tennis—in everything—in the postwar years?

Well, yes and no. It is certainly true that the serve-and-volley game demanded superb conditioning. We were about to cease hearing and reading of players collapsing on the sidelines or in the dressing rooms after playing a long, important match. But that was in itself no bad thing. It merely placed tennis on equal footing—at least—with the other major sports, where it had long since been expected that world-class players would be physically able to respond to extraordinary situations as they arose.

Nor was the Big Game itself evidence of declining mental power among the top players. Far from being evidence of a new crudity, it actually represented a thoughtful refinement of the game. Mercer Beasley, a famous coach of the twenties and thirties, had divided the court into three zones for his pupils. The baseline and the area behind it was a red zone and from it one made no attempt to hit winners. The percentage play was to hit a high shot that cleared the net and landed well away from the opponent's sideline and baseline. The best one could do from the backcourt was to maneuver a bit, hoping to move up into the amber zone between the service and baselines, where one's hopes of getting a sharp angle for placement improve, even as the distance to the green, or attacking zone in the forecourt, shortens. It is up there where the chances for placements improve, because the chances for hitting a sharply angled, unretrievable shot also greatly improve. All the Big Game did was get the player up into that green zone quickly, without the falderal that had previously attended that activity.

Of course, there was more to it than that. At some point Kramer and his pal Schroeder encountered an engineer named Cliff Roche who, though not much of a player himself, had gone to the trouble of calculating what the "percentage shot" was in almost every conceivable tennis situation. This enabled them to simplify, simplify, simplify—to know in advance what shot they must hit in reply to anything an opponent might throw at them, thus eliminating the distraction of thumbing rapidly through a mental card file of alternatives. This was an enormous advantage because, as Kramer once said, "There is no time to think on a tennis court; the less you think the better off you are." He went on to say that he always hit an approach shot to the place on the court where he had the best chance of keeping it in, even if he knew full well that his opponent was on his way to precisely that point. The thing was to hit your best shot and force the man across the net to deal with it, thus putting the pressure on him to bring himself up to your best level, or level best.

Kramer was entirely open about what he was doing. For example, he publicly stated that he would always return a short forehand down the nearest line, giving

111

his opponent just two alternatives: a backhand back down the line, where Kramer would be awaiting it, or the shot he—everyone—knew was one of the toughest in tennis, a short, cross-court backhand. Either way the percentages were with Kramer.

The same thinking went into the Kramer serve. He was as strong as Vines or Budge in their prime, and he was as capable as they were of banging a ball past an opponent with sheer speed. Generally speaking, however, both his first and second serves were moderately paced balls. The primary effort was not to ace his opponent, but to pull him off court, beyond the sidelines, where his best riposte was the low-percentage cross-court shot which Kramer could put away with a crisp volley. If the man managed a decent stroke along the sideline, Kramer himself went for a cross-court stroke, but deep to the baseline-sideline corner farthest from his opponent.

Kramer (and Roche) believed it was foolish to have too many shots to choose from in your arsenal—"It is better to have one good shot and use it repeatedly than to have two or three"—and they did not believe in going all-out to break an opponent's serve every time. The percentages lay with holding your own serve at all costs and waiting for the other fellow to get himself into trouble when serving, then to apply pressure, using those reserves of strength one gathered by taking it easy in most receiving games.

It was—it remains—a brilliant system. Indeed, there is no alternative to it at the highest levels of play. The only people who could give Kramer a decent game were those who could take the net from him and force him to play a defensive, baseline game. In fact, as we shall see, no one ever did learn to beat him consistently. As planned, he joined in the 1947 defense of the Davis Cup, then turned pro. Thereafter, in one long touring series after another, he defeated all comers until he retired to promote the tours himself.

His game does, however, present some problems. At first, as Kramer admitted, the public did not understand serve-and-volley tennis. As he put it in 1955: "It's boring. Someone serves, comes into net, and either makes a good volley or forces an error. Occasionally a perfect passing shot is made. There are no backcourt maneuvers; the groundstroke artists don't win."

It worried him, but he thought there were only two things to do about the matter: "either change the game or interest the public in volleying tennis." The former, as he admitted, meant fooling around with the basic rules of the game—making the server stand, say, two feet behind the baseline, or requiring both server and receiver to wait one stroke before being allowed to cross the service line. The latter possibility, getting the public to acquire "the deep knowledge of the game" which would allow it to properly appreciate the new strategy, seemed to Kramer, twenty years ago, even more difficult than changing the rules.

Yet as things worked out, a certain knowledgeability about and appreciation of the Big Game did evolve. The reason was simple: It was good show business. It is fun to see someone combine accuracy with speed while serving, even more fun to see the possessor of such a weapon come wheeling to the net behind it and deliver a crushing volley. There is fast action and a show of violence, and that, for better or worse, puts tennis in tune with the times. Moreover, the brisk, high-speed, quickly finished rallies of modern tennis suit our shortened attention span.

Finally, we cannot help but feel a certain awe and envy as we watch a Connors, a Laver, a Newcombe on our television set. Just looking at them we know in our aging, aching bones that we cannot hope to emulate them, that they are playing tennis at a level entirely beyond our reach. Of course, that is true of the baseliners of yore, as well, but we did—and do—play their game, or attempt it. It does not compel the wonder that this fast yet finely tuned modern game does. In short, it seems to me unlikely that tennis would ever have become the popular spectacle it now is if Kramer, disciple Schroeder, and theoretician Roche had not, in effect, reinvented—or perhaps more properly, restyled—the game in the late forties. There are, indeed, tennis historians who are a bit sniffy about Kramer's credentials as an immortal, since his career as a

113

competitor in the great amateur tournaments was so brief. This, however, takes an extremely narrow view of his accomplishments. By the time he turned pro he was intelligent enough to see that there was no one left on the scene who could do more than take the odd match from him. More important, he must have realized that his game had established itself as *the* game at the top levels of the sport, that there was no point in continuing to prove the obvious (especially since his heir, Schroeder, was on the scene and would win Wimbledon in 1949, in his only assault on that championship, as well as lead the successful American defense of the Davis Cup). For a time, in fact, the rest of tennis was caught in a cultural lag. Veteran players were still playing the old game which Kramer so easily dominated, while the newer generation—at least in America—was not quite ready to challenge Kramer at his own game.

Indeed, while Kramer was establishing his mastery of the amateur world, two of its prewar greats were trekking up and down the land, reestablishing the professional game and, incidentally, giving a final demonstration of classic tennis. They were Don Budge and Bobby Riggs. They were perfectly cast. The tall, gentlemanly Budge looked the part of a heroic figure, and his game was heroically proportioned. Riggs, of course, was Riggs, with an accurate but not overpowering serve and perhaps the most consistent return of serve in the history of the game. Annoyingly, he returned everything the big fellow could throw at him, winning a war of attrition, but by no means winning the crowd.

These were the first great tennis players I ever saw, and Budge was the first ever to talk to me ("Hey, kid, get me an orange drink; and have one yourself"). And, as it happened, he won the night they pitched their canvas court on the basketball floor of the old Milwaukee County Auditorium, which pleased me no end, since my father had taught me that there was something not quite sporting —perhaps not even entirely masculine—about Riggs' style. Budge's was not *the* Big Game, but it was big enough and it was difficult to understand why he was having so much trouble with Riggs. The latter has since claimed that a note

of caution crept into Budge's game as he himself crept into his early thirties, that he was not going for the lines with quite the audacity he had in the days of his greatness.

Be that as it may, the fact was that on that winter night in dim and drafty old County Auditorium, one had the feeling that one was caught in a time warp. The reputations of Budge and Riggs were made before the war, and though they were still—even by the odd standards we apply to athletes—young men, one thought of them somehow as has-beens. In part, this was because professional tennis, played on endless tours, in settings more appropriate to such disreputable sports as boxing, had in those days a tacky air about it, something distinctly second class compared to what we imagined Wimbledon or Forest Hills to be. In part, however, this sense of being present at a sort of animated antique show derived from newspaper accounts of Kramer's doings, an impression that out there in the great tennis world revolutionary things were happening, that this new man with his new style of attack could beat any man in the house.

We were being unfair. All too well had the tennis establishment put over the notion that professionals were pariahs, betrayers of the amateur ideal, vulgarly cashing in (in an appropriately seedy atmosphere, symbolic of their sell-out) on reputations made in purer venues. (It was not until many years later, when I sampled the genuinely disgusting tone of Forest Hills, that I came to understand that, whatever its rigors, touring might be preferable to that circus of hypocrisy in Queens; at least the players were isolated from officious swells, wearing badges and lecturing them, like children, on what was "good for the game." It was, manifestly, a hard dollar they were making, but it was an honest one.)

Riggs convincingly defeated Budge on both their 1946 and '47 tours, then won a tournament designed to select Kramer's first opponent when he turned pro. Indeed, their very first match, in Madison Square Garden, on December 26, 1947, was an omen of things to come. It coincided with one of the city's great blizzards, something like two feet of snow having fallen in the twenty-four hours

before curtain time, paralyzing public transport. It looked as though Kramer's debut would take place before an empty house. This, however, reckoned without the passionate interest of the basic tennis nut. They straggled through the deserted streets, some on snowshoes and skis, to witness what many of them undoubtedly believed would be the birth of a new tennis era. (No player before Kramer had turned pro when his game was so obviously at the peak of perfection.) And though the supporting cast—Dinny Pails and Pancho Segura—played their preliminary to empty seats, by the time Kramer and Riggs took the court, the arena was nearly filled. Here, obviously, was a market of undreamed of, and untapped, potential. It is a measure of how blind and slow of foot the tennis establishment has been that more than two decades elapsed before it began to adequately serve that market with open tennis.

Riggs won the first match, mainly by surprising Kramer. He recklessly charged the net, serving and volleying in the very manner on which his opponent was supposed to hold exclusive patent, varying that strategy only by throwing up more than the usual number of lobs, difficult to see as they came down out of the Garden's lights. After thirty matches in their cross-country series, the heralded Kramer was only two games ahead of Riggs, 16-14. Thereafter, however, the older man was able to win only six matches, and Kramer ended the touring season with an astonishing 69-20 edge. "Playing Kramer night after night was like pitching a World Series game," Riggs has written. "My arm began to wear out from the constant serving and volleying at maximum speed and power. Kramer was bigger and stronger and gaining in confidence all the time."

His experience was to be repeated time and again on the pro tours. Pancho Gonzales fell to Kramer 96-27, Segura went down 64-28, and Frank Sedgman, the Australian winner of the 1952 Wimbledon, did scarcely better against him on the American's final tour as a player. Kramer was convinced that the best tennis in the world was played in these marathons, that every top amateur who volunteered for a cross-country set of tennis lessons from

116

Gonzales, a Chicano from Los
Angeles, taught himself tennis on
public courts with a 50-cent
racket his mother gave him, hoping
to keep him out of trouble.
He practiced relentlessly (as below)
and blossomed in late 1940s
as heir apparent to Kramer. He
lost at Wimbledon (opposite)
in 1949, but won two U.S. titles and
teamed with Schroeder
to win Davis Cup. Soon thereafter
he turned professional.

him emerged a better man for the experience. They all learned what Riggs instinctively understood before stepping on court for the first match in the Garden: that the only hope was to try to take the net away from Kramer—and such success as they enjoyed resulted from the employment of that tactic.

Most never learned, however, the full value of percentage tennis, namely, not to overplay the ball. Falling behind Kramer they would "try too tough a volley or too good an approach shot, instead of being content to throw the ball back" and wait for the put-away shot on which the percentages were more favorable to them. Premature pressing for an advantage, not sheer exhaustion, was Riggs' downfall, according to Kramer.

It was certainly, in the larger sense, the downfall of Richard "Pancho" Gonzales. Or perhaps, in a way, it was the making of him as the modern player possessed of the most potent legend. When Kramer left amateur tennis, Gonzales was his heir apparent. Moreover, as a Chicano born and raised in Los Angeles, he was the first member of a minority group to reach the top levels of the game—at a cost that he has hinted at in the majestic (sometimes sullen) aloofness of his manner and the unflagging ferocity of his competitiveness, but never openly discussed. What happened to Gonzales was simple. He won the U.S. title in 1948 and '49, and in the latter year teamed with Schroeder to defend the Davis Cup 4-1. Both men won their singles, Gonzales in straight sets. Then, at twenty-one, having won no other major championships, he turned pro, in part because Schroeder backed away from the contract offered by Bobby Riggs, who was now promoting a tour to star his friendly former foe, Kramer.

It was Kramer who suggested that they go after the youthful Gonzales, but it was the fast-talking Riggs who caught the same plane Gonzales was flying from New York to Los Angeles and emerged from the cabin, many hours later, with the young man's signature on a contract. By any standards, Gonzales at this point was premature in his decision to turn pro. He was, in many ways, an untutored youngster. He had learned his game, with no coaching

whatsoever, on the public courts at Exposition Park in Los Angeles, playing at first with a racket his mother had acquired for fifty cents and which she hoped would help to keep him from becoming a juvenile delinquent. It did, though his love for the game did turn him into an habitual truant—so frequent an offender that the ineffable Perry Jones finally prohibited him from playing against his other prize juniors on the grounds that he had an unfair advantage over youths whose practice time was confined to the after-school hours.

Like Riggs before him, he received few of the best perks which his regional association was capable of bestowing on him, and people remember him on his first tour of the eastern grass-court circuit, living in rooming houses, grateful to get a free meal at a tennis writer's home. Thus, he had no reason to want to linger among the amateurs. But if his time at the top was no less than Kramer's, he was not the seasoned player—or for that matter, the mature individual—that his first professional opponent had been when he made the jump. In the interval between winning Forest Hills and turning pro, he lost a number of tournaments (like the Pacific Southwest, which he had been expected to win, and which earned him the sobriquet, "the cheese champion." This led fellow players to nickname him "Gorgo"—for gorgonzola).

Truth to tell, his performance against Kramer was cheesy. He lost their tour 96-27, and found himself a player without a home. The amateur circuit was barred to him, and there was no living to be made as a performing professional, his box-office value having dropped as a result of his sorry record against Kramer. The latter went on recruiting the newest amateur flashes to beat up on, having taken over the promoter's as well as the star's role, and though Gonzales continued to develop—he won the national professional tournament for the first time in 1953—he did so in painful and ill-paid obscurity. That victory, however, the first in a record series of eight consecutive wins in the only decent tournaments the pros had, was the beginning of his rehabilitation.

The following year he defeated Pancho Segura

Lean, handsome Vic
Seixas (below) encountered
Australians at the peak of their
Davis Cup power in 1950s,
endured six losing years out
of seven on U.S. team. Trabert (r)
shared four of them. His
best year was 1955, when he
won three of four Grand
Slam events, missing a chance at
Australian title by losing
semifinal match to Ken Rosewall.
Rosewall? 1955? Yes.

124

and Frank Sedgman in a tour that was set up on a round-robin basis, and then Kramer signed him to meet Tony Trabert on a new *mano a mano* tour. In 1954 and '55 Trabert had won three of the Grand Slam titles, adding in the process a second U.S. title to his record, and Kramer doubtless sensed that he would have a tough time against the smooth-stroking, steady-tempered, and much younger player. He also had observed that despite a lack of constant, top-caliber opposition, Gonzales' game had finally peaked. Indeed, it was even better, perhaps, than the shrewd Kramer realized, for he humiliated Trabert 74-27.

That, however, was fair enough, for Gonzales himself had been humiliated by the terms of his contract for the series. Trabert had received $95,000 for it, Gonzales a $15,000 pittance. By 1958, Gonzales, who had gone on to beat Ken Rosewall and Lew Hoad (and would go on to master Rod Laver when he joined the professionals) was still playing gin rummy with Kramer, but he would not speak to him as they picked up and slapped down the cards. Indeed, Gonzales never travelled with his tour mates, preferring to hit the road alone, setting his own pace in a fast sports car that he fussed over with more tenderness than this abrupt, moody, put-upon man could find in his heart for most human relationships.

Yet painful as his time of testing must have been, it had in the long run some salutary effects. His lonely trail made him, for people who really cared about tennis, a legendary figure of heroic proportions. Kramer was, after all, a guileful, clever man off the court as well as on. It was too bad he could not have gone on playing his brilliant tennis in open tournaments, but he was quite visibly doing all right for himself—and not merely financially. He might, for example, constantly raid amateur tennis for its latest flash, but even while doing so, Kramer seemed somehow to maintain excellent relations with the amateur game's leaders. At the same time, he continued to keep the warily affectionate regard even of perpetual disestablishmentarians like Riggs.

Gonzales, however, is not, never has been, clever in these ways. He did not find his reason for being in the great world of tennis, but in the chalk-marked rectangle that should be, but often is not, its heart. He was born to play, not to politic, and there was a ferocious purity in his commitment to the game itself that was, finally, awesome—analogous in a way to that of Ted Williams' similarly fierce (and similarly misunderstood) commitment to the essence of his chosen sport. Athletes of this sort are very rare and they are generally the victims of bad public relations. Each sport, at its top level, is a closed world and the player who wishes to win popularity contests is generally careful to keep his contemptuous feelings about noncombatants—the controlling interests and their handmaidens, the press which regularly covers the game—to themselves. In this little world, good-fellowship is the key to a good image and it takes a very long time for genius that does not choose to express itself fraternally to win through.

Gradually, however, it began to come over people in the late fifties and early sixties that though Wimbledon and Forest Hills champions might come and go, Richard A. Gonzales had been for a long time and was continuing to abide as the best tennis player in the world. Tennis writers he had not bothered to cultivate might cast doubt upon the "trenchancy" of his groundstrokes—principally because his serve and his net play were so powerful that he did not have to resort to them often—but anyone with an unprejudiced eye could see the quality of

The Pros: In 1950 at Madison
Square Garden (from l): Pancho Segura,
Gonzales, tour manager Bobby Riggs,
Frank Parker, Kramer. Far l: Trabert,
being welcomed to pro ranks by
Gonzales in 1955, was walloped by
Kramer as decisively as Gonzales had
been. Bottom: Gonzales (prone,
after rushing net) in final
set of 1969 Wimbledon marathon
with Charlie Pasarell.
Pancho won in five sets which
required a record 112 games.

his character as well as his game. There was the magnificently efficient serve, so beautifully functional; there was the pouncing quickness of his movement on the court, that inevitably sent sportswriters to the big cats (lions, tigers, pumas) for similes and metaphors; there was the canniness of his defensive skills when age lessened the sting of his offensive game. Finally, the fact that he had never won Wimbledon, that he had never attempted a Grand Slam, that he had perfected his skills in high-school gyms and war-memorial auditoriums during brief stopovers that punctuated endless, lonely freeway miles, didn't make any difference anymore. No matter what strange fires he had tempered his talent in, no one could in the final analysis dispute the quality of that talent.

But Gonzales was more than a legend. He was a necessary player in the historical sense. For as he went on and on down his lonely victorious road it became more and more absurd that a young man with no wealth but the cunning of his racket hand should be forced into the cold because he could not afford the decent, but only modest, rewards of the shamateur system, especially in a period when the great stars of other sports were finally being rewarded with a fair share of the money their gifts generated at the box office. It is impossible to say precisely what the example of Gonzales meant in the long fight for open tennis, but the glamour that began to surround him, the sense of sharing his frustration that came over many of us, surely meant something. And when open tennis did finally arrive, he majestically justified our faith in him.

In 1968, when Wimbledon was finally opened to the pros, Gonzales was forty, too old to expect to win so grueling a tournament. But the following year he entered the record book anyway by engaging twenty-five-year-old Charlie Pasarell in the longest singles match in the tournament's history: 112 games, requiring five hours and twelve minutes, spread over two days, to complete. It is a record that will never be broken, since the following year Wimbledon adopted a tie-breaker system, and it was a characteristic Gonzales performance. They went on court a few minutes before six o'clock in the evening, on June 20,

and promptly got into a first-set wrangle that lasted well into the gloaming; Pasarell finally pulled it out after eleven set points 24-22. With darkness gathering, Gonzales thought that was enough, but the referee decreed otherwise and a fuming Pancho threw the next set 6-1.

Next afternoon the marathon resumed, Pasarell saving seven set points before finally losing 16-14 on a backhand that missed the baseline. Confidence renewed, and with Pasarell perhaps letting up in the belief that the old gentleman would tire if the match went to a fifth set, Gonzales took the fourth 6-3. He looked quite done in, leaning on his racket between points, flicking perspiration from his brow. But somehow he hung on and with the game score standing 8-9 against him, Gonzales rallied and took eleven consecutive points and the match 11-9. The last point—need one say it—was a service ace. He shuffled from the court exhausted, the cheers reverberating around him. "I'm a little tired" was all he would allow himself to say in the dressing room. Again the analogy is to Williams, stroking a home run on what he and everyone else knew would be his last time at bat in baseball.

Except that Gonzales has yet to quit. In 1971 he won the Pacific Southwest over a field that included, among others, Jimmy Connors and Stan Smith. In 1972 he won $10,000 in less than two weeks, reaching the finals of one tournament before losing to Pasarell, then jaunting on to Jamaica, where he won a Rothman's Spectacular, defeating Clark Graebner in the finals. In his mid-forties, he dominates the so-called Grand Masters tour and still enters other major events when the spirit moves him. In them, he remains capable of beating any of his juniors when his game is just right or theirs is just off. It is good to see him there, back where he belongs. He asks no quarter from his opponents, expects no allowances from those of us in the stands who are drawn to his matches, not out of pity or false nostalgia, but because his is an irresistible court presence. As with the aging Olivier on the stage or the aged Rubinstein at the piano, one comes away not merely pleased to have been in his company, but further instructed in the subtleties of an art.

127

San Francisco

an album
of notable courts

Field courts, Forest Hills

Newport Casino, RI

Homestead, Hot Springs, VA

Longwood Cricket Club, Boston, MA

Overview of Wimbledon

Kooyong, Melbourne, Australia

St. Moritz, Switzerland

Stade Roland Garros, Auteil, France

Forest Hills in 1970s

the phenomenon of australia

Determined Jack Kramer gave a certain stability to professional tennis. Once he became proprietor of the pro tour the amateur establishment could count on his staying in business, almost annually raiding their ranks for each new star who gathered celebrity by winning Forest Hills or Wimbledon, or performing suitable heroics in Davis Cup competition. He was, of course, a nuisance, but his approach to professionalism was not as radical in its effect on the game as his tactics on the court had been. His tours, after all, were based on old "Cash and Carry" Pyle's model and were but a better-financed version of the professionalism that had been familiar since Tilden's days.

No, what really changed tennis in the fifties and sixties was not an individual effort, but a national effort —Australia's. Since 1950, the Aussies have won the Davis Cup sixteen of the twenty-four times it has been contested, and a player from Down Under has, in the same period, won Wimbledon fourteen times and Forest Hills fifteen times. Even on French clay, a surface not suited to their game, they have won ten times. No other nation has come close to matching that record. Nor has any nation, at any time in the history of modern tennis, produced a chain of champions as strong as that forged in Australia in the last quarter century. Frank Sedgman, Ken McGregor, Mervyn Rose, Lew Hoad, Ken Rosewall, Neale Fraser, Ashley Cooper, Mal Anderson, Rod Laver, Roy Emerson, Fred Stolle, John Newcombe, Tony Roche—they seemed to hand the major championships down to one another like the members of a large family passing along the clothes they had outgrown or become tired of. And again, like a numerous clan, they battled mightily among themselves for prizes, but let some outsider come along and challenge them on some important matter—like the Davis Cup—and they instantly banded together for mutual self-defense.

Occasionally, of course, someone (usually an American) made inroads on the Australian monopoly of world-class tennis, but this was nearly always a case of individual talent briefly triumphing over organization. No nation, during the final two decades of amateur dominance of the game, developed a coherent program capable of tak-

ing the play away from the Aussies for a sizable period of time.

On the face of it, there was nothing very complicated about what the Australians did, nothing that other nations could not, in theory, emulate. All they did was make an earnest effort to discover talented players at a youthful age, ask them to devote themselves single-mindedly to the pursuit of tennis excellence, condition them superbly, and then send them forth to play for their country all over the world. In the United States in the midfifties, when it became clear that the nation was going to be only accidentally competitive with the Australians in Davis Cup play, a good deal of effort was put into developing a junior program that would find and develop talent in the Australian manner, but not a great deal came of it, certainly nothing like the success the Aussies enjoyed.

It was particularly frustrating because the nonplaying captain of the Australian Davis Cup team, Harry Hopman, was not in the least secretive about his training methods. He was always happy to send copies of the program he had used to bring Hoad or Rosewall up to the highest international standard to an inquiring coach, and when these arrived in the mail or were published somewhere, they always turned out to be somewhat less complex than the plans for the H-bomb. Indeed, they seemed to consist of little more than a requirement that the players do a good deal more roadwork than most tennis players were used to (in order to develop stamina), and perhaps play a bit of squash to develop quickness.

Hopman did develop a two-on-one drill in which a player was forced to play alone against a doubles team peppering shots at him from every angle—a sadistic little exercise that developed stamina and quickness simultaneously and which has since become a standard part of the top players' training regimen. Still, with players around the globe earnestly doing their roadwork and employing Hopman's training techniques, very few were able to measure up to the standards the Australians set during the fifties and sixties, and so it becomes interesting to examine more closely what was happening in Australian ten-

Opening pages: Ken Rosewall symbolizes the great Australian tennis tradition, in part because his remarkable career spans its entire modern era. Below: His splendid contemporary, Lew Hoad, in one of his famous Davis Cup matches against Tony Trabert. Temperaments and careers of these competitors and teammates could not be more contrasting. Steady Ken is still winning. Injuries forced Hoad's retirement while he was still at top.

Top: Greatest Australian doubles
team was Adrian Quist (l)
and John Bromwich, who won national
title eight years running.
Frank Sedgman, toweling off after
a tournament win at age 43,
was most "decisive" player after
Kramer. Two scenes from 1952
(center & bottom): Whipping Drobny
at Wimbledon, defending U.S.
title successfully against Gardner
Mulloy. Two-handed driver with tongue
aslant is Bromwich at age 16.

nis in those days—particularly since it now seems that the Aussies themselves are no longer able to duplicate the successes they enjoyed in those years.

Arthur Ashe, who may be the most thoughtful (as well as the most arrogant) of the great contemporary players, believes that Hopman was the right man in the right place at the right time, that his methods could not and would not have worked as well anywhere else at any other time. Australians are, to begin with, an extraordinarily athletic people, perhaps because their nation's remoteness and essentially agrarian economy do not encourage intellectual and artistic pursuits. Aussies, by their own definition, are, as Ashe says, "mutton punchers" and "sodbusters," which is a way of saying that they place a high value on the frontier virtues of uncomplaining endurance and courage. Or at least they did in the years of their greatness. This, basically, is what Hopman understood about his countrymen—that you could ask more of them in the way of rigorous discipline and vigorous training than you could of young men who were the products of a softer society, offering more amusements and distractions than Australia did a quarter of a century ago, even perhaps a decade ago.

These young men had character, and Hopman's hard, sometimes high-handed methods developed it further. Through the years they have been regarded as rather colorless by tennis writers and fans, only because they were, as a rule, not flamboyant in their behavior on the court, not very exciting to interview after a match (if, indeed, Hopman, who liked to control everything, allowed an interview).

On the other hand, they had, by and large, admirable temperaments for the game. They might occasionally glare lingeringly at a linesman who made a close call against them, but they rarely threw a racket or a temper tantrum. Nor did they ever offer physical ailments as an excuse for bad play. The credo was simple: If you had an injury you defaulted, ergo, if you did not default you were not hurt. Or, as Roy Emerson once put it, "You walk on the court, you have no excuses." (The obverse of this was a certain contempt for players who constantly argue that it

was a pulled muscle or an aching tennis elbow that brought them down. "I've never beaten him when he was well" is the Australians' standard, contemptuous remark about players whose constitutions develop sudden delicacies when they are beaten.)

By the same token Aussies are never admittedly homesick (though it is known that John Newcombe, among others, suffers acutely, if silently, from this illness). Because of the remoteness of their native land and the infrequency of major tournaments there, they must spend more time in faraway places, among strange-sounding accents, than any other group of players and are thus, perhaps, more entitled to this emotion than anyone else. But again, that is not the sort of thing a man talks much about. (It is perhaps no accident that Rod Laver's favorite recreation is western movies, especially those featuring that great stoic, John Wayne.)

Instead, the Aussies band together more tightly than players from the other countries do, are mutually supportive in a way that is quite remarkable considering the competitiveness of their occupation—and the fact that in the small world of big-time tennis they constantly end up playing against their "mates." This does make them the best team-tennis players in the world, remarkably cooperative in their efforts to win or defend the Davis Cup or the new World Cup. They seem honestly puzzled by someone like Jimmy Connors, who won't play for his country just because he doesn't happen to like the coach. Hell, most of them didn't much care for Hopman, come right down to it, but that was no excuse for not joining the team.

They had, these men who were known, whether they liked it or not, as Hopman's boys, a sense of pride in themselves as individuals and as representatives of a team and nation that they carried onto the court with them—and which, in turn, carried them through a lot of tough spots. No matter how tired they were, they refused to show it. At the changeovers they walked and breathed easily—no slumping, no visible signs of exhaustion. And if they happened to fall behind, they continued to exude confidence, a sense that they would pull back to deuce, maybe even ace

137

Whiz-Kid Time: Hoad and
Rosewall (r) flank Aussie mentor
Harry Hopman after returning
from their first international tour
in 1954. Below: On their way
to the Italian doubles championship
early in the trip. They also
won French and Wimbledon doubles
and both reached the singles
semifinals at Wimbledon.
Rosewall also won the French
singles, a feat he would have to
wait fifteen years to repeat.

you in the process, and then go on to win the game, the set, the match. Which they often did. All any of them seem to remember Hopman saying to them when they were behind in a tough match was "Go for the lines"—hit out, that is. Don't play cautiously. Play your own game.

For all of that, they are pleasant, open men. Their idea of a grand time—their *only* idea of one according to some bemused opponents—is to drink vast quantities of beer together in noisy camaraderie. Not that they are clannish about it. Just about anyone is welcome to join them, as long as his "arms aren't too short or his pockets too long" to "shout"—that is, to buy a round. They are, obviously, perhaps determinedly, plain in their pleasures and this personal conversation extends to dress ("neo-Good Will," as Ashe, who can sometimes be seen leaving Forest Hills in a cool dashiki, puts it) and to a shrewd, ceaseless pursuit of the cheapest lodgings, the most inexpensive meals when they are on tour. Indeed, their tightness is a legend among the pros and is, of course, a product of the straitened, lower middle-class circumstances which almost all the great Australian players have as a common background. ("What was your biggest surprise in tennis?" a reporter is alleged to have asked Pancho Segura, or some other veteran of the tour. "The time Ken Rosewall picked up the check," he is supposed to have replied.)

Besides being one of the tour's sure-fire standing jokes, the Aussies' tightness reveals something important about them and the reason for their overwhelming success in international competition. To be sure, a general athleticism might be expected in a country that is remote in location, rural in character, and climatically suited to outdoor activity. And, yes, games of all sorts, fostering a general joy in competitiveness, are likely to attract kids who don't have a wide variety of other, tonier recreations to choose from. And, indeed, Hopman had a fine national tennis tradition to build on—one to which he had contributed as a player and which reached back to Davis Cup victories prior to World War I. And, yes, tennis fortunately had never been an exclusive, country-club sport in Australia. It had always been as open to talented kids as, say,

football is in England and the United States. And yes, yes, yes, Hopman was a man whose Spartan training methods grew naturally out of, and thus admirably suited, what for want of a better term we might call national character. But he could not have worked the wonders he did if there had not been a large pool of ambitious, unwealthy young men who saw that for the few he chose international tennis was one of the very few ways out of the dull and dreamless life that Australia generally offers its youth.

Rod Laver has been very frank on this point. He says that when he was breaking in, making his first tours as a junior, the Americans he played were every bit his equal, even occasionally his superior. Incomparable as Laver may be, it seems evident that somewhere along the way, under the Aussie system, he got better, while his equals and superiors, training the American way, did not.

At age fifteen the Australian youth completes all the education the state mandates for him and is generally expected to start earning a living. College is not, for the majority, a realistic option. What happened to a promising young player in Australia, in the days before professionalism, was that he was given a make-work job with one of the sporting-goods manufacturers, a job that gave him all the free time he needed to practice and to tour the big tournaments. These jobs were, by standards prevailing outside the peculiar world of tennis, exploitative; they paid just enough for a modest living and their continuance was dependent on the player's remaining malleable to Hopman's instructions, which extended to matters that had little to do with tennis—table manners, for instance, and etiquette, enforced with fines for gaffes. Hopman was not infrequently criticized for being a petty dictator.

Indeed, he was and indeed the players were, like Olympic competitors from the Iron Curtain countries, subsidized and, therefore, by any standards professional athletes. Their freedom to concentrate totally on tennis, while their chief rivals, the Americans, were forced to maintain at least a show of merely avocational interest in the game —dutifully pursuing their college educations and taking their pay in the form of inflated "expenses"—was the major

Rosewall skates into
a backhand at Wimbledon in
1968. As always, the
title eluded him
when he lost in the semis.
He was a finalist in
1954 (losing to Drobny),
1956 (when Hoad beat him),
and in 1970 and '74
(when Newcombe and Connors
won). He is the greatest
player never to win
the greatest tournament.

reason for Australia's dominance in the fifties and sixties.

Obviously, it was their freedom to concentrate on the game that enabled Hopman to develop those innate, uniquely Australian traits of character which have continued to serve his players so well in the age of the professional, and long after he emigrated to America and ceased coaching the Australian internationals. Equally obviously, the endless, year-in, year-out success of the Australians had its effect on world tennis, playing its part in generating pressure for redefinition of the term "amateur." Indeed, it seems significant that Hopman was extremely resistant to open tennis, understanding that once young players were free to support themselves by tournament winnings, they would not be willing to submit to his velvet-gloved tyranny, that without his control over the only source of income available to his players—the sporting-company jobs—he could not control their training or the development of their games, that, therefore, Australia would inevitably lose the edge it had enjoyed until then.

His fears have, in fact, been justified. Since the coming of open—that is to say, professional tennis (no amateurs get very far in a major tournament) in 1968—Australia has become just another tennis power, having won but one Davis Cup since that year and very often finding such odd-lot countries as West Germany and Rumania, India and Japan reaching the finals ahead of it. Meantime, on the international circuit it is the Australian veterans—Newcombe, Laver, Rosewall, and the rest—who maintain the national honor. There are no Australians in the top ranks of the newer arrivals, none to rank with Connors, certainly, or with his hard-charging contemporaries—Björn Borg, Guillermo Vilas, Vitas Gerulaitis (representing, respectively, Sweden, Argentina, the United States).

Yet it was a great reign, unprecedented and unlikely to be duplicated again, since among its other desirable effects professionalism has drained much of the nationalism out of tennis. The top players now play essentially for themselves, and constitute a little nation unto themselves, the only significant nation, indeed, governed on anarchist principles. This is not surprising, considering that everyone with a significant voice in its affairs grew up under the yoke of some sort of athletic fascism.

Be that as it may, the man who made the Australian Davis Cup team run on time, after four humiliating defeats by the United States when competition resumed after World War II, was a man who, like all the power-minded El Supremos of the political world, believed in getting his subjects young, before their minds and temperaments were fully formed, indoctrinating them in his philosophy before they were softened by more indulgent methods. Harry Hopman had, of course, been a world-class player of the second rank before the war and nonplaying captain of the team that had won the cup for Australia in 1939. Others managed the nation's defeats in the cup matches of 1946-49, though in the last of those years a youngster Hopman was helping to develop was included on the team and played respectably in losses to Ted Schroeder and Pancho Gonzales. His name was Frank Sedgman, a small, wiry blond, notably quick on the court and with his smile—the latter being particularly appreciated by newsmen and spectators, who were used to a more dour manner among the leading Australian players.

In 1950, with Hopman again in the captain's chair, he decided to play Sedgman, whose conditioning he and his trainer, Frank Findlay, had directed toward the development of muscular power to complement his speed, in the number one singles spot. More important, Hopman went with young Ken McGregor as the number two singles, in effect declaring a new era in Australian tennis. Of the veterans, only Bromwich was used in the challenge round, teaming with Sedgman to win the doubles, with the latter winning both his singles matches (against Schroeder and Tom Brown) while McGregor took his singles against Schroeder, the Aussies thus winning the round 4-1.

That was the beginning, and it is impossible, without devoting an entire book to this era, to recount all of the Australians' triumphs in the years following. The next year, Sedgman teamed with McGregor to win an unprecedented and so far unduplicated doubles Grand Slam. It

The places change, as do
the cut and color of the togs,
the surfaces of the courts,
the tint of the balls,
the numbers of the years,
but the adversaries
seemingly go on forever.
Below: Laver (foreground) and
Rosewall face each
other still another time
in their 78 x 36 foot
arena. Opposite: Rosewall,
no longer young, but capable.

was not until a year later, however, that he won one of the major titles outside Australia, in the process becoming the first man from Down Under to win the U.S. title. He played throughout the tournament, in the words of one journalistic witness, "the most decisive tennis of any man since Kramer," losing only two sets (to Trabert in the quarterfinals) as he marched past, among others, Billy Talbert, Art Larsen, and finally Vic Seixas. The same year he finally won Wimbledon, defeating Jaroslav Drobny (who had beaten him in the French finals) and sweetened the triumph by winning a triple—taking the doubles with McGregor and the mixed doubles with Doris Hart. He went on to defend his American championship successfully, beating Gardner Mulloy in the finals in straight sets, then climaxed the year by leading his country to a 4-1 defense of the Davis Cup, winning his singles against Trabert and Seixas, and teaming with McGregor to beat them in the doubles.

Only a purse collected by solicitation through Hopman's newspaper had kept him an amateur this long, but now there was no resisting Jack Kramer's blandishments, and Sedgman's brief, brilliant career at the top of the tennis world ended immediately after the Davis Cup challenge round—as did McGregor's.

His defection to professionalism, however, had more effect on Coach Hopman's reputation than it did on Australia's success in Davis Cup competition and major tournament play. Sedgman and McGregor had been ranked first and third in the world when they went professional and their places in those positions were taken, next year, by Trabert and Seixas. It did not seem possible that the Americans would return from Australia without the Davis Cup, for the team Hopman decided to throw against them was a pair of nineteen-year-old Sydney natives, Lew Hoad and Ken Rosewall, who had been playing each other for years in the junior ranks. The former was a muscular, scowling, forbidding player, the latter a small kid with an unprepossessing serve (perhaps because he was a natural left-hander forced to play righty by his father), what was to become, by common consent, the best backhand in the game, and—not as often remarked upon—an absolutely superb volley, unspectacular because at his height it did not come crashing down on a hapless opponent in a way

that awed spectators. What they did not notice was that the little man was—and remains—uncannily proficient in being in position to employ it and uncannily accurate in his placement of it.

Be that as it may, in 1953 it looked as if the powerful Americans would pulverize the Australian youngsters. Although Rosewall had won the Australian and French championships earlier, he and his partner had both lost to their Davis Cup opponents in the U.S. semifinals. Still, things started out well enough, with Hoad upsetting Seixas in the first match, Rosewall losing to Trabert. Then, however, under pressure from his selection committee, Hopman substituted Rex Hartwig for Rosewall in the doubles, breaking up a solid team only because of Rosewall's first-round singles loss and because he had not looked sharp in practice. Seixas-Trabert took the untried pair with the loss of one set.

Now, with press and public vocally critical of the doubles gaffe, it was up to Hoad to keep the Australians alive in the series by beating Trabert. The match began under overcast skies and before long it was raining. The first set required sixty-five minutes to play, longer than any previous match of the meeting. Hoad finally broke Trabert with a passing shot to take the set 13-11. Suddenly confident, Hoad took the second set behind a flurry of service aces 6-3. Now the court was soaked and first Trabert, then Hoad, donned spikes—the latter for the first time in his career. The American was more used to this footwear and was, in any case, a canny campaigner. He began slicing his approach shots and the sodden balls scarcely came up off the grass at all. Digging them out, Hoad was lofting his returns right into Trabert's deadly volleys and the American took sets three and four easily, 6-2, 6-3.

Then, early in the fifth, two accidents turned the match around again. Going after a sharply angled Trabert winner near the net, Hoad forgot he was wearing spikes and tried to end his lunge with a slide. His feet caught in the turf and he crumpled at Hopman's feet. The master psychologist flipped him a towel and some kidding remark about being a clumsy oaf. Hoad grinned and laughed and suddenly the tension was broken.

Not long thereafter Hoad's racket was broken as

145

Among the many "greatest matches ever played" must be included the brilliant and grueling battle between Laver and Rosewall for the professional "World Championship of Tennis" at Dallas, TX, in 1972. With some 21 million TV viewers looking on and a $50,000 prize at stake, these two protean players hammered each other for five prodigious sets that took nearly four hours to play.

he socked a return at Trabert, and the replacement turned out to be a much more effective weapon. The broken one, its gut soaked by the rain, had not been giving him the power he was accustomed to commanding.

The new racket gave him aceing power, and suddenly he had a 6-5 lead, Trabert to serve. Somehow Hoad got him down love-30. Then Trabert missed his first serve, Hoad adjusted his position to receive the second serve and his slight motion threw Trabert off, causing him to double fault. The partisan crowd in Melbourne's Kooyong Stadium cheered—most unsporting. Triple match point. Trabert served to Hoad's backhand. Hoad chipped it back, hopping like a lawn bowler trying to will his ball into good position. Somehow it cleared the net, and although Trabert flung himself desperately at the ball his return went into the net and the match belonged to Hoad.

It is said that it took hours for both players to calm themselves after what many believe to have been the most emotional Davis Cup match since Budge-von Cramm. In tears, the normally agreeable Trabert excoriated the crowd for cheering his double faults. "They're a pack of animals," he cried. But it was no use. Rosewall, perhaps inspired, perhaps just his quiet, competent self, put Seixas away with the loss of just a single set shortly thereafter and the cup was safe in Australia for another year.

Trabert, however, had nothing to apologize for thereafter. A year later he and Seixas were back in Australia to challenge for the cup. Trabert whipped Hoad, while Seixas reversed the previous year's results against Rosewall. Then they clinched the cup by winning the doubles. At the ceremonies when the cup was presented to the Americans, Trabert made handsome amends to the crowd for his cross words of the previous year, and the following season he had his best year ever, winning Wimbledon, the French and the U.S. titles, as well as the U.S. indoor and clay-court championships, an unprecedented display of versatility on a variety of surfaces. It is fair to say that in this period he was the only man to approach the great Australians in consistent quality of play.

Hoad, however, was not to be denied his time of greatness. Teamed with Rosewall, he regained the Davis Cup in 1955 and defended it in 1956, winning both challenge rounds without the loss of a game. In the latter year, he defeated Rosewall for the Australian title, Sven Davidson for the French title, and Rosewall again for the Wimbledon crown. He had but to win at Forest Hills to have a Grand Slam, but Rosewall outfoxed him, coming on with a strong attacking game—not his style at all—to win in four sets.

The following year the muscle spasms and back injury which had begun to plague him a little earlier were particularly troublesome, but his defense of the Wimbledon title was masterful, requiring only fifty-six minutes to demolish Ashley Cooper, the Australian who would win Wimbledon the following year, 6-2, 6-1, 6-2. Many regard this, his final match as an amateur, as the greatest of his career.

There was about him then, as always in his career, a "tempestuous majesty," in John McPhee's fine phrase, that made him a compelling figure. Indeed, playing hurt, he did better against Gonzales on tour than anyone else did, perhaps succumbing in the end not so much because the American changed his grip, but because physically he—Hoad—simply could not stand the pace. Indeed, many believe that if Hoad had stayed well open tennis would have come ten years before it did, so compelling and crowd-pleasing a figure was he, so much was his fiery figure missed at the great amateur championships. Comfortable as the owner of a successful tennis ranch in Spain, he has nevertheless missed the huge prosperity and the large fame Rosewall has enjoyed as he continued to play in the top-flight open tournaments. He tried a comeback at Wimbledon in 1970, only to lose in an early round to the Egyptian El Shafei. Even so, perhaps his best epitaph was spoken by his pro touring partner, Gonzales. If there were a universe Davis cup, he is said to have remarked, and you had to pick one player to play one match for the world, you would want Lew Hoad in his prime.

So, his great career is touched with sadness. As is that of his great contemporary, Rosewall. He won his first major championship in 1953, when he defeated Mervyn Rose for the Australian title, which he regained again in

The Gamest of Tries: Rosewall
(l) gives it his all in 1970 while
carrying Newcombe to five sets
in Wimbledon finals. But Newk (c)
got the silverware. Set scores
were 5-7, 6-3, 6-2, 3-6, 6-2. Right:
Famous Newcombe serve as it
appeared to his opponents before
he slightly improved its —
and his — ferocity with his excellent
mustache. Also missing:
The fierce glare he fixes on
victims before cranking up.

At Forest Hills in 1974.
"I wish he'd hurry up and get old," said Newcombe, just before being upset by Rosewall in semifinals. Alas, Jimmy Connors aged him quickly with an overwhelming straight-set victory — the shortest men's final in the tournament's history. Rosewall has since claimed to be semiretired, although continuing to win his share.

right—but only because Rosewall has turned out to be such a remarkable athlete. Yet it may be, ironically, that that 1954 final also was Rosewall's best chance at the title. The next time he reached Centre Court at the end of a tournament, it was to meet his old friend and rival, Hoad, at the top of *his* game and with *his* Grand Slam chances very much alive. As he had Drobny, Rosewall extended his opponent to four hard sets yet lost; Hoad was at his irresistible best.

Coming off that good year, Hoad was resistant to Jack Kramer's professional siren song, but Rosewall, ever on the lookout for money, submitted to it, and then submitted rather ignominiously to Gonzales, who was at the top of *his* form on their tour. Gonzales, however, made him a better tennis player, his best weapon against the hard-hitting American being the quickness he developed in getting to net and bringing his ever-improving volley into play.

When Gonzales retired in 1960, Rosewall dominated professional tennis in a period when it lacked a colorful star personality, thus suffering the irony of having his game peak at a time when no one was paying much attention. These were the years when, if there had been open tennis, he would surely have won Wimbledon. Indeed, after Rod Laver won his first Grand Slam in 1962 and turned pro, Rosewall (and Gonzales) regularly defeated him on their tour.

What adds special poignancy to the Rosewall record, however, is that in a period when the contemporaries of his period of youthful triumph have all retired, and even the fine Aussies who came after him—the likes of Ashley Cooper, Neale Fraser, Roy Emerson, and Fred Stolle—are at best making token appearances in the major events of the tennis world, Rosewall is still a contender. Consider: At the first-ever open tournament at Bournemouth prior to the first all-comers Wimbledon of 1968, amateur Mark Cox grabbed the headlines by defeating two famous professionals, Gonzales and Emerson, while most people have forgotten that the winner of that event was quiet, steady Ken Rosewall.

They forget too that Rosewall established what looks as if it will be an unbeatable record by winning the

1955 by beating Hoad. In 1953 he also won the French title and three years later added the U.S. title to his paragraph in the record books, in the match that robbed Hoad of his Grand Slam. These, along with his Davis Cup successes, made him one of the premier players of the world and, of course, a logical candidate for a Wimbledon victory.

Indeed, he had an excellent shot at that title in 1954, when he reached the finals against Jaroslav Drobny, the Czech without a country and a man who, since 1949, had been a perpetual semifinalist (and once a finalist) at Wimbledon. The crowd belonged to Drobny on that June day when he and Rosewall met, the feeling being that this might be his last good chance for the title, while the young Aussie had plenty of time. In a peculiar sense, they were

Australian title in 1971 (he successfully defended in 1972), a full eighteen years after he had won it for the first time. Similarly, there were fifteen years between his first French title and his most recent one in 1968, fourteen between his first and second U.S. championships. Perhaps more significant, he has won, from Laver in both instances, the World Championship of Tennis final tournaments, each carrying a $50,000 paycheck, in 1971 and 1972, when he was thirty-six and -seven. At thirty-nine, in the summer of 1974, he was again a finalist at Wimbledon and at Forest Hills, this time with the crowds very much on his side. Somehow the fact that in both instances he lost quickly (it was the shortest U.S. final on record) to the brutal efficiency of Jimmy Connors seemed less important to some of us than the remarkable fact that a man we could think of as a contemporary was there at all.

"The least appreciated great player in the history of tennis" is what Rod Laver calls him and he is entitled, finally, to due recognition—a recognition this recessive personality has never seemed to seek—as an immortal. Old timers, says Laver, tell him all the time that Tilden "would cut us all down with his groundstrokes, but there's no way I'll believe Big Bill could bomb out little Kenny from the baseline." And what sensible man would disagree with that judgment?

What one most admires about Rosewall, finally, is the unobtrusiveness, the sheer lack of pretentiousness, of his game. There are guys on every club court in the world who serve harder than Rosewall, and where most world-class pros have at least three different ways of hitting a backhand, Rosewall's slice is hit only one way—"perfect," as Arthur Ashe says. What's great about his game are things it requires a certain sophistication to notice and appreciate. His speed coming to net is obvious, for example, but it takes a while to get around to noticing the perfection of his footwork, which is what gives his shots their instruction-book quality. His lob is wonderful, but even more wonderful is his way of disguising it. Finally, there is his uncanny court sense, his ability to anticipate his opponent's placement of shots and to be there waiting for it.

This, of course, is coupled with a wonderful accuracy in his own shot making. When he is on he seems to be moving the man across the net around with a tiny, powerful magnet concealed somewhere on his person.

But it is more than just a similarity in age that makes some of us identify so powerfully with him. When we watch a Connors or a Newcombe or a Laver it is obvious from the first moment that we are watching players who are in a different league from any we have ever known or aspired to. Rosewall, however, lacks the blessing of special endowment, even as you and I. It seems he has taken ordinary weekend tennis and by dint of enormous concentration and intelligence raised it to remarkable heights. He doesn't do anything we couldn't hope to do if we had his will, his drive for perfection, his unflappable temperament.

Manifestly, we will never achieve what he has achieved, but of all the great players, he is probably the one from whom we can learn the most, the one whose achievements are, at last, receiving the recognition that they have for too long been denied. At Forest Hills in 1974 I made it a point to watch as many of his matches as possible, and the thing that perhaps impressed me most was the way he looked when he stepped off court after three or four or five hard sets, sometimes against players half his age. He had the appearance of a man who had just stepped from an hour or two of the kind of mild exercise the doctors prescribe for middle-aged gentlemen—a pleasant stroll on a suburban sidewalk, perhaps, or weeding the garden. One thought of something Ashe had said during a press conference: "'Muscles' just mows the lawn on you." One can only be grateful that Muscles survived, better than most, the years of wandering in the pro tennis wilderness, that he is still capable of winning in tennis' brave new world, thus enjoying—as so many of his Australian contemporaries have not—the prosperity they who brought world-class tennis to new levels of excellence deserve more than most. "He has to be," says Ham Richardson, a contemporary who is now an investment counsellor and sometimes competitor in senior tournaments, "one of the remarkable athletes of our generation."

151

7

age of the professional

He is a small, modest, quiet-spoken man, quite unremarkable in appearance or manner—except, of course, on a tennis court. Some people even say that he is surprisingly insecure psychologically. Close up, what one may notice first about Rod Laver is his left forearm. Hugely overdeveloped from hitting a million, two million—who knows how many?—tennis balls with his uniquely wristy topspin, both forehand and backhand, it is brightly freckled and so hard-muscled that it put writer John McPhee in mind of a Dungeness crab.

In motion, of course, it is his quickness that rivets the eye. At his best a few years ago it was generally believed that he was faster on the uptake and, again because of the potent flick of his wrist, better able to stroke the ball powerfully while on the run than anyone who ever played the game. Reflexive speed of Laver's kind doubtless begins with a natural gift, but it is said that early training had a great deal to do with the height to which it was developed. He began his tennis career by batting a ball against a garden fence at his family's home, a ranch (or "property," as the Australians have it) in Queensland. Because of the toll this took on the paint and the nearby flora, he was told to build himself a practice facility that posed a smaller threat to the local ecology. His work was no masterpiece of carpentry, but it had a singular effect on his game, for the balls he hit against it rebounded in highly eccentric fashion. Pursuing them, he developed his remarkable ability to not merely defend all corners of the court, but to turn what would be, for another player, merely a good get into an attacking opportunity.

What may be less obvious to the spectator, given the calmness of Laver's manner, is the ferocity of his competitive instinct, but it is this quality which has made him a legend among his fellow players at tennis' top level. That, too, is something that goes back to his earliest training. His first coach was a man named Charlie Hollis, whose belief was that every player should aim for a perfect match every time out—6-0, 6-0, 6-0 being, of course, perfection. He noted, wisely, that an awful lot of tennis matches are lost when the man ahead thinks his margin is safe and relaxes,

either out of pity for his opponent or out of a desire to save energy for the next day's action. Obviously, even Rod Laver cannot win every match by such a margin, but it is nearly impossible to think of an occasion when he has let up—even when his cause was obviously lost. What his fellow pros remember most vividly is the number of times they have taken a set from him only to find themselves blasted off the court 6-0 in the next set.

Thus the basic personality of the great player of the sixties, arguably the greatest of all time. He is the first man since Don Budge to win the Grand Slam and the only man in history to win it twice. He is the only tennis immortal whose career was not fatally disrupted by the disjunction between the amateur and the professional game—his first slam having been won when the great tournaments were exclusively amateur affairs (1962), his second coming a year after they were opened to the pros.

Laver has made his career look easy, but he claims, with some justification, that it was harder in the doing than it looks in retrospect. His family moved to Rockhampton, a town of some 30,000 population, in part because his father had done well enough on the ranch to justify semiretirement, in part because the father wanted his three sons—all of whom showed a gift for the game they practiced, not merely against a bangboard, but on a court they made themselves—to get some proper coaching. The elder Laver did not believe his diminutive youngest son had either the physique or the natural gift that the other boys had. But there was something about his quietly determined air and his even temperament that Hollis thought suited him for the game, and it was he who not only taught him the foundations of his mature style but brought him to Hopman's attention in the late fifties. Hopman, among other things, gave him his nickname, the Rockhampton Rocket, shortly to be shortened to the Rocket.

"He was the Rocket because he wasn't," Hopman has said. "You know how those nicknames are. Rocket was one of the slowest lads in the class. But his speed picked up as he grew stronger"—as a result of the gym work Hopman, as usual, prescribed, and as a result of Laver's newly

Opening pages: The Rocket
fires. Occasion is one of his
less happy Wimbledons —
1971, when Newcombe won the
title. Below: His most
happy Wimbledon — 1962, when
he defeated Aussie Marty
Mulligan in straight sets to win
title and third leg on
first of his two Grand Slams.
Mulligan had almost
beaten him in French finals
earlier in season.

Great Moments on Centre Court.
Clockwise: Laver receives his first
Wimbledon Trophy in 1961 from
Princess Marina. He carries it off
as Tony Roche, his victim in
1968 final, acts the good sport. He
shoulders trophy he retained
by beating Newcombe on 1969 final.
In action against Roche in
1968 match. Right: Serving in first
professional tournament ever
permitted at Wimbledon.
Year was 1967 and Laver won.

acquired habit of carrying a tennis ball everywhere and squeezing it constantly, which was the beginning of his extraordinary wrist power. Good, willing kid that he was, he was picked for Australia's international touring teams starting in 1956, building no more than a fair to middling record until in 1959 he played an historic eighty-three-game semifinal at Wimbledon, beating the powerful American Barry McKay to enter the finals against Alex Olmedo, who handled him handily.

Now, obviously, he was a comer. Laver himself began, prematurely, to entertain fantasies of a Grand Slam in 1960, when he beat his countryman—and the world's first-ranked player—Neale Fraser for the Australian championship, which was held in Brisbane, Queensland's capital, and which was among the most satisfying of Laver's wins because he was only the second native of that state to win the national title. There was, however, to be no slam that year. Indeed, there were no more major titles for a year and a half, until he beat Chuck McKinley of the United States in straight sets for the first of his four Wimbledon titles, a modern record.

That first Wimbledon win convinced him he was as ready as he was ever going to be, and he was quite open about going for the slam the next year. Indeed, the Australian championships set the tone for 1962, since there (as in France and the United States) he met his fellow Queenslander and best friend, Roy Emerson, for the title. Emerson, himself a remarkable player, extended him as far as anyone—save one curious character—did that year, taking him to four sets here and at Forest Hills, five in the French finals. Even so, it was not Emerson who posed the greatest danger to the first of Laver's slams. It was another Australian, Marty Mulligan, the only player (as it turned out) in any of the slam events to hold match point on Laver.

That was in the quarterfinals of the French tournament, played on the soft clay of the Stade Roland Garros in the Bois de Boulogne. Laver, along with the majority of the other best players, believes that the French open is the toughest leg on the slam, because the serve-and-volley game they like best is simply not suitable to this surface. It was right, however, for Mulligan, a small, steady Aussie. As frequently happens with players of the second flight, he was in the middle of one of those streaks where, for a few weeks or months, he was playing above himself and entirely capable of knocking off his betters. In this instance, Mulligan took two of the first three sets and had Laver down 4-5 and 30-40 in the fourth. Laver saved the match point by anticipating that Mulligan would maintain his pattern of sending his backhand return of serve down the line, where Laver cut it off with a sharp volley. From there he went on to hold serve and the game score reached 8-8 without a break. Meantime, the volatile French crowd, hoping to see an upset, and betraying their customary national prejudice in favor of the artful clay-court rallier, swung vociferously behind Mulligan.

When Laver was serving in the seventeenth game, however, he hit an approach shot that even he seems to believe sailed over the baseline. The line judge, however, called it in and Mulligan erupted in uncharacteristic rage. He slammed a ball at the linesman, and screamed at the umpire and at the tournament referee who appeared on court to try to calm the situation. The upshot was that he lost both his concentration and the support of the crowd. Laver took that game and the next, and then won the deciding fifth set at 6-2. He was almost out of the woods though he says both Neale Fraser and Roy Emerson, his final opponents in the tournament, had excellent chances to beat him. But both became cautious, hesitant, when they had the edge on him, Emerson indeed having a two-set lead on Laver after two sets had been played in the final. As for Mulligan, he again emerged on center stage—indeed, onto Centre Court—as Laver's opponent in the Wimbledon final, where the Rocket dispatched him in three easy sets.

Thereafter, Mulligan settled in Italy, where the clay courts suited his game and the money to be made as a paid participant in the interclub matches that are popular there suited his pocketbook. Indeed, in one of those bizarre twists that were common in the world of shamateur tennis, he was chosen to represent his adopted country in the Davis Cup competition a few years later, and his former Aussie

Pioneers of Professionalism: George MacCall (opposite), whose National Tennis League was underfinanced and often disorganized, but gave women their first good chance to play for pay. Left: Lamar Hunt, whose wealth and tenacity made World Championship Tennis a viable proposition — and broke shamateurism's stranglehold on the game.

mates took to referring to him as Martino Mulligano.

Still, he did provide Laver with the highest hurdle on his otherwise comparatively smooth road to the Grand Slam which included, incidentally, wins in the national tournaments of West Germany, Switzerland, Holland, Norway, Ireland, and the British Hard Court.

After this feat, the opportunity to turn professional was irresistible, and the fact that Laver did so in 1963 may well have saved professional tennis and thus made open tennis—just five years later—possible. The problem the pros faced was that they had not been able to sign a major box-office attraction since Hoad in 1957. Everyone knew that Laver was the man who could revitalize the game, and even Gonzales, then in retirement, offered to come out and meet Laver in a series of head-to-head matches, guaranteeing him $50,000 and extending the possibility that he might make as much as $100,000 if he could win consistently. Laver, wisely, was afraid of the old lion—on balance, a winner on every one of his post-Kramer tours—and also felt a certain loyalty to his fellow Aussies—Rosewall and Hoad, who guaranteed him $110,000 over three years for a series of round-robin matches with them. It was an open secret that the older players didn't have that kind of money, that they might have to scratch very hard for it if the addition of the Laver name to theirs did not bring the people in. It did, however, and in the long run the old masters helped measurably to polish Laver's game to a high sheen. In particular, he mentions the development of a much-improved lob, which was amusingly effective in the often tacky arenas where they set up their canvas courts for one-night stands; very often you could loft a ball up among the rafters where your opponent lost sight of it!

Touring, of course, had its character-strengthening aspects as well. In Khartoum the troupe played amid a revolution, and at night they were subject to a "bug curfew." When the lights attracted too many insects, and the court became squishily unplayable, the event simply ended, which didn't bother the crowd at all, since the Sudanese were used to having outdoor evening entertainment summarily suspended by this nuisance. In La Paz, the thin air of the altitudinous Bolivian capital brought them near collapse. And in St. Louis, Missouri, they played a noon exhibition of doubles on a court marked out in the middle of a downtown street to publicize their for-real matches that evening. It was tough going, but Laver had become infected with his tour mates' "belief that if we could just keep going someday pro tennis would thrive as a significant sport."

There was, in fact, less time to wait than he and the others, stroking so hard to stay afloat in this athletic backwater, imagined at the time. Indeed, it is generally believed that 1964 provided a significant turning point. There had been a U.S. professional tournament since 1927, when it was played on a vacant lot in New York, but as late as 1963 a field of just eight players had been mustered and only one of them, Pancho Gonzales, ended up getting paid for his trouble. As the biggest gate attraction, he had had the foresight to insist on a $100 guarantee—in advance—for his appearance. The winners collected nothing, because receipts were insufficient to cover expenses, let alone the announced prizes.

One year later all that was suddenly changed. A bank—that respectable bastion of all that is most square and conservative in our lives—agreed to underwrite the U.S. pro tournament if it were held at Longwood, near Boston. A prize purse of $10,000 was guaranteed.

This had a miraculous effect on the professional game, for with the Longwood tournament as an anchor, a little string of tournaments at convenient locations along the East Coast could be organized, offering total prizes amounting to some $80,000. Three years later Wimbledon for the first time permitted professionals to tread the sacred grass in a tournament that was both artistically and financially successful (Laver won the final from Rosewall).

Not long thereafter a promoter named George MacCall organized something he called the National Tennis League, for which he recruited most of the veteran touring pros. The idea was not to play a marathon series of one-night stands, but to play a series of brief tournaments

159

in a variety of locales for solid, if not yet spectacular, prizes. The reminiscences of his players suggest that MacCall was not perhaps the best-organized tennis promoter who ever lived, and that he was perhaps a tad underfinanced. Nevertheless, he was visionary enough to recruit four fine women players (Billie Jean King, Rosemary Casals, Françoise Durr, and Ann Haydon Jones) to his tour in 1968, giving them their first decent opportunity for professional play. (Georgeous Gussie Moran—she of the lace-panties fame—and Pauline Betz had toured unsuccessfully for Bobby Riggs in 1950–51, and later the great Althea Gibson and Carole Fageros—also known as "The Golden Goddess"—had toured, playing matches as preliminaries to Harlem Globetrotter basketball games, with no known good effect on the gate.)

At around the same time a man named Dave Dixon, who was bankrolled by Lamar Hunt, Dallas oil heir and a power in professional football, attempted to emulate MacCall. Although MacCall beat him out of most of the established pros, Hunt was willing to finance a mass raid on the amateur ranks. Now the amateur establishment was confronted not with the loss of one or two replaceable first-line players, as in the past, but with the possibility of mass defections by *all* of their top attractions. Unless they sued for peace, the great amateur tournaments, and the circuit of less prestigious tournaments that connected them, would come to be what the colleges had become for professional football and basketball in the United States: minor-league training grounds, interesting and even profitable in their way, but manifestly not representative of the game at its best. The old order might, perhaps, have stood off MacCall, but it was quite clear that Hunt had the patience and the wealth to wear them down, especially after he and Dixon parted company and the Texan recruited a top-flight group of sports-management experts to guide his interests from day to day.

Moreover, amateur tennis, just at that moment, had a lot to lose. There was, for example, Roy Emerson, Laver's great contemporary and, in the eyes of some knowledgeable tennis people, the holder of an even more impressive record than Laver. He had never won all the Grand Slam tournaments in one year, but he had won more of them across the years than any other man in history: a record six Australian titles and two apiece of the other great championships. Moreover, in a decade of Davis Cup play, he lost only one singles match (to Manuel Santana, in 1965).

Perpetually boyish, perpetually fit, he was in his prime, a literally gleaming player, his hair slicked down and shiny as patent leather, his gold-filled teeth flashing at his opponents as he dashed netward, faster perhaps than any other player. His physical condition was a byword. People remember him running four miles on the morning of days he was due to play difficult matches, and perhaps varying the routine by leaping a hedge five feet high and two or three feet across. He was not a guileful man; there wasn't even much topspin on his groundstrokes, nor were there canny variations in the pace of his game as the character of a match changed. Everyone said he was the life of the party off-court and, in a way, it could be said that he was the life of the party on it, as well. It is perhaps to be expected that it was "Emmo" who devised one of those little conveniences that mean so much to the hard-working pro; for it was he who was the first to cut the pockets out of his tennis shorts, thus eliminating a few ounces of dead weight he no longer had to carry about with him in the course of his high-speed maneuverings. Emmo perhaps waited too late to make the move into professionalism, but, as he said, for him the money was still awfully good in the amateur ranks and perhaps the wide-ranging sociability of amateurism appealed to him more than the gloomy, sealed-off lives of the pros in pre-open times, when they wandered the world in search of a buck with only each other—endlessly—for company. (The troupe that played Khartoum's bugs split $1,000 four ways for their effort.) Fred Stolle, Emerson's partner in so many Davis Cup competitions, a fine doubles player, winner of Forest Hills in 1966, and a three-in-a-row runner-up at Wimbledon, may have been in the same category. But there were others whose games were just beginning to peak when the hard-headed visionaries of professionalism approached them.

Perhaps the most important of their catches was the 1967 Wimbledon winner, John Newcombe, whose game had been steadily developing throughout the sixties, but there were other bright young men on hand to give the professional game a depth it had never had before: the gifted Tony Roche (to whom injuries have denied greatness), Cliff Drysdale, Nikki Pilic, Roger Taylor—all of whom abandoned amateurism for Hunt's World Championship Tennis tour.

Before long, the WCT absorbed the NTL, and before long it also abandoned the radical method of totting up points it briefly embraced at the beginning—the Van Alen Streamlined Scoring System, which was basically an extension and modification of that used in table tennis. About this curiosity a word ought to be said. It was the brainchild of an upper-class eastern-seaboard gentleman who was convinced that the reason tennis had not achieved mass popularity was because its traditional scoring system was too complicated, too exotic, for the unwashed to cotton to. It apparently never occurred to him that the reason the game he loved had not spread further was because the establishment brethren had kept it in a straitjacket. There is, of course, rich irony in the fact that it was the *arrivistes* from Texas who gave the VASSS its first extensive trial and discovered that it simplified all the drama and suspense right out of the game.

Be that as it may, the emergence of WCT posed a singular threat to tennis' traditional way of doing business. Although there were those in the International Lawn Tennis Federation, citadel of fogeyism, who favored a fight to the death, it was the English Federation, controlling the world's premier tournament, which led the fight to finally accommodate the game to the basic trend of athletics in this century—that is, to an open admission that no game can be played at its top levels by any but those who devote their lives to perfecting their play, that such devotion is no more nonsensical (and often much more pleasurable) than any of the other occupations (politics springs to mind) that serious people seriously devote themselves to.

Threats to suspend the English association from the International body and to prohibit amateurs who competed in the English open events from competing in other ILTF-sanctioned events did not materialize, and the world's first open, the British Hard Court Championships of 1968, produced its famous surprises, with amateurs like Cox defeating pros like Gonzales and Emerson, but no scandals. Its winner, Rosewall, went on to win the first open French national tournament. Laver won Wimbledon so commandingly that his final opponent, Tony Roche, was quoted as saying that he spent most of the match looking for a hole he could crawl into and hide. Only Arthur Ashe, still technically an amateur, upheld the honor of those honor-bound not to accept pay for play, winning Forest Hills by outlasting Tom Okker in the finals.

So tennis' divided house was in the final stages of collapse, but neither the players nor the public cared. They could clearly see a fine new mansion rising to replace it. Indeed, it seems that Ashe missed his Forest Hills paycheck only because he was waiting to see who would give him the best offer for turning pro.

Of course, the ILTF didn't see it that way. It now became apparent that it had gone along with the English because it imagined that if the big tournaments it sanctioned offered suitable prizes, the players would be satisfied and drift away from the permanently floating, exclusively professional tournaments. There was also a feeling in the Association that the public itself would get tennised out by being offered too much of the game, causing the WCT to collapse under the weight of its heavy expenses. Over the succeeding years, much maneuvering ensued, all of it confusing to the public and tedious to recount.

Moreover, the ostensible issues kept shifting. First the ILTA said it would not pay the fees the WCT demanded when it permitted its players to appear in ILTA-sanctioned events. (This is what led to the all-amateur——and unaffiliated pro—Wimbledon of 1970.) Then there was a hassle about scheduling conflicts between the two organizations. This became a particularly nasty business when something called the Grand Prix arose and flowered. Obviously it was a major attempt to compete

162

with the WCT without seeming to. The idea was a kind of tournament of champions, the field to be composed of the players who piled up points awarded on the basis of their performance throughout the year at ILTF-sanctioned tournaments, many of which—how odd, old chap!—conflicted with WCT events.

Meanwhile, just to make things more interesting, women professionals were getting themselves organized and making difficulties for the ILTF, too—a matter to be taken up in more detail in the next chapter. And a men's players association was born and quickly grew strong, so strong indeed that it actually struck Wimbledon in 1973, protesting the banning from it (and other ILTF events) of Nikki Pilic, who was being punished for refusing to play Davis Cup for his country (Yugoslavia) because it conflicted with his WCT obligations.

In short, it was a fine kettle of tennis sneakers. And yet, despite all this juvenilia, the game prospered.

There were fine young players like Ashe and Stan Smith coming up and, most important, there were the old pros, who quickly followed Rosewall and Laver in finding their bearings again in the rigorous context of long, exhausting major tournaments, something some of them had not seen for a long time.

It might have seemed that John Newcombe would emerge from the crowd first. After all, he had won the last all-amateur British and American national tournaments, and he was a young man whose game had grown in an unforced, natural sort of way. And he was perhaps as physically powerful as any man who had ever played the game, thus better able to withstand the demands of a suddenly, vastly expanded schedule. Yet, oddly, he had to wait his turn while thirty-one-year-old Rod Laver made history.

Suddenly, quite unexpectedly, in 1969 Laver had a second chance at a Grand Slam, and once again those close to him knew he was going to go for it, fully aware that

time was creeping up on him, that his chances for accomplishing this feat would inevitably diminish with each passing year. This time, as he must have known from the start, it would be no walkover, since this time *all* the best players would be present at all the major tournaments, including the likes of Rosewall and even Gonzales, who had not been in a position to challenge him his last time around.

It was almost over for him before it began, in the semifinals of the Australian open, in the blistering heat of Brisbane, playing Tony Roche. After three sets the scores were 7-5, 22-20, and 9-11, Laver leading, but with the psychological edge favoring his younger opponent who, overall at that point, had beaten the Rocket more often than he had lost to him. Coming back as he had—mostly because his return of service was superior—in that third set in this match of near-record length, made all the difference psychologically as the players headed for their intermission showers. Indeed, Roche returned to court at the top of his 165

form, reeling off five straight games before Laver finally held service. At this point, of course, he knew the set was gone, but it was important for him to win that sixth game in order to serve first in the fifth and deciding set. Form, he says, was completely forgotten (by him at least) at this point. His only hope was to scramble and hack, try to stay even with Roche, and hope that either Tony would cool off or that the breaks would start going against him. And so they did with the game score in 4-3 in the Rocket's favor, but with no breaks recorded and Roche serving. Then, serving at 15-all, he watched a backhand chip shot of Laver's sail cross-court and, to the best of Roche's knowledge and belief, out. Even Laver is not sure, to this day, that it was in. He was just not in position to see it clearly. But the linesman called it good. Roche (like Mulligan in Paris seven years before), exploded, lost his concentration and the game, and, a few minutes later, set and match. The final, against Andres Gimeno of Spain, was a mere formality—a straight-set win for Laver.

Surprisingly, so was the French championship. Of his seven opponents, only Tom Okker of the Netherlands was able to take a set from Laver on this alien soil, normally so uncongenial to his game. In the final against Ken Rosewall, the defending champion and a player one has to like better than Laver on clay, Laver had one of those days when everything goes right. He kept the ball so deep, and hit it at such a good pace, that Rosewall had no chance to close with him, either by gobbling up weak second serves or making the kind of approach shots that would allow Rosewall to employ his devastating volley.

Wimbledon, however, was tough. Here Laver was not going merely for the third leg of the slam, but for the modern record of four Wimbledon victories, perhaps the most unique of his achievements. He seems to feel that his most difficult match was in the fourth round against Stan Smith and, indeed, it was the only match of Laver's tournament that went five sets. Laver took the first two fairly easily, but then Smith began attacking more strongly behind his serve and even on Laver's, and he took the next two sets, the scent of victory growing more powerful for

him with each winner he hit. In the final set, he had a great chance. Laver says he had to serve from behind in every one of his service games, and though he got an early break himself, to lead 3-1, he was not out of the woods. At 5-3, serving for the match, he found himself down 0-40 and thinking that a break "would have put wings on his [Smith's] confidence." Laver did not believe he could have fended the young American off if he had lost that game. But, of course, he didn't. He rose to the top of his form, took five straight points and the match.

He had some trouble with Arthur Ashe in the semifinals, with Ashe—a streaky player—hitting one of his hot spells to blast Laver in the first set, scaring the Rocket badly, since Ashe has been known to be unbeatable for three sets when his game hits one of these peaks. Luckily for Laver he cooled as quickly as he heated, losing the next set badly, rallying to extend the third to 9-7, then simply collapsing to lose the concluder without winning a game. This victory sent Laver into a match that many believe to be one of the key contests in recent tennis history, his final against John Newcombe. Newk had won the tournament in 1967 and he would win it again in 1970 and '71. Thus, if he could have taken this match, he would not only have robbed Laver of his chance for a second Grand Slam, but would himself have become the first modern to hold four Wimbledon men's singles titles. It might have made him a superstar, on a par with Laver in his own sport and, perhaps, tennis' answer to such multimedia celebrities as Muhammad Ali and Joe Namath. In any event, it would have taken the curse off his own career, which stems from the fact that he stands at the end of a long line of Australian tennis stars, a breed with which everyone appears to be jaded.

But it was not to be. And it may be that it was a single missed shot that cost him this status—or so Lew Hoad, among others, believes. Laver won the first set, but then Newcombe took the second, and had broken out to a 4-1 lead in the third, and was ahead in the sixth game, when he needed a backhand down the line for a sure winner.

"But," as Hoad has said, "Newk can't hit a backhand down the line. He had to slice it cross-court, and

John Newcombe — he of the
drooping shoulders and drooping
mustache — has an excellent,
crowd-pleasing game and
personality. He has won almost
everything in sight
(although he lost TV extravaganza
to Connors), but generates
less excitement than he might
if he were not simply
the most recent in a too-long
line of superlative
Australian champions.

Rocket was there."

That single point gave Laver life. He held his serve and clawed back to win the set, and the fourth and final one, by identical 6-4 scores. In the retelling, he makes the final leg of the slam, Forest Hills, seem almost anticlimactic and, indeed, only Dennis Ralston, Emerson, and Ashe extended him at all in that tournament. In the finals, delayed by rain and played on a slippery court, he donned spikes to win fairly easily over Tony Roche, who was favoring a pulled leg muscle and was afraid of injuring himself so seriously he would not be able to continue if he put on spikes. (They prevent a player from gliding into his strokes and cause dangerously sudden stops and twists.)

The slam, of course, made Laver very rich. That year he became the first tennis player ever to win more than $100,000 in a twelve-month period and, a little later, he became the first man ever to win a million dollars in the course of a career that is not yet over. These well-publicized winnings were important to the game, because they called attention to the fact that it was now, however belatedly, a big-money sport, like golf, like all the team sports to which we pay the most attention. Yet Laver, like most of his countrymen—Hoad was the exception, as previously noted—is a rather colorless chap, not the kind of man who comes across wonderfully on television or in interviews, is not, in short, a personality with star quality.

Neither, of course, was Rosewall, who in 1971 and '72 defeated the Rocket for the richest prizes in tennis, the WCT final championships in Dallas, which carry a $50,000 first prize. (The second of these meetings, a five-set, three-hour-and-forty-five-minute match, nationally televised, is regarded as a grand classic confrontation between a heavy serving attacker—Laver—and a brilliant counterpuncher, Rosewall. But Rosewall, for all the sweetness of his personality, is a hero only to near-geriatric cases like the writer.) Arthur Ashe, were he a more consistent player and less preoccupied by the obligations imposed on him as tennis' only black star, could have been the great central figure the game needed, but he has only two major championships to his credit. Stan Smith, hero of the U.S. Davis

Cup victory before hostile crowds and grossly unfair officiating in Bucharest, Rumania, in 1972 and victor in the Wimbledon finals that same year against the comical, crafty, yet artful Ilie Nastase—his most dangerous tormentor on his trip behind the Iron Curtain—has seemingly lost his winning touch prematurely and, in any event, is such a dully earnest sportsman that he makes the Aussies look like movie stars.

No, the best hope among the men was Newcombe, with his drooping shoulders and mustache, his hugely powerful and therefore crowd-pleasing game, and his excellent nature. On the court, as writer Frank Deford has said, he is wonderfully attractive, "so game, so competitive, playing nearly possessed" when he's on, yet capable as well of the odd humanizing lapses that make us identify with his troubles and soar with him when he wins. Off the court he is, sometimes, as fellow player Dick Stockton said, "a thirty-year-old boy," yet easy to take to heart, "utterly at ease, almost lacking in ambition except to obtain those dull, small comforts of middle-class security—to be with his family, to provide for his old age, to have a few beers now and then, and a lot of beers now and then, too." (The description is again Deford's.)

In short, he was the nice guy who combined an exploitable personality with a great record (three Wimbledon, two Forest Hills, an Australian, and a WCT title so far), a man who needed only that extra little something—that fourth Wimbledon title—to overcome the handicap of being the last in a too-long line of Australian champions. He knows it, knows that he is, in the world's eyes, just an in-betweener, the solid player who in the history books will be the man between Laver and the game's next dominant personality—God help us, it may be Jimmy Connors. Or, alternatively, that he may be recalled as the best male player of the Billie Jean King era, she being the personality around whom the social history of the game revolved in the late sixties and early seventies. It is too bad. He deserves better. But he certainly teaches us the value of being able to successfully hit a backhand passing shot down the line when we need it.

169

parity with men

Here is a capsule history of women's tennis: In 1919 Suzanne Lenglen won the first of her five consecutive Wimbledon titles, beginning the process by which she established herself as not only the dominant player of her sex, but one of the dominant sports personalities of her era. In 1966 Billie Jean King won the first of her three consecutive Wimbledon titles (she has added two more since 1968), beginning the process by which she established herself as not only the dominant player of her sex, but one of the dominant sports personalities of her era.

Between the Age of Lenglen and the Age of King, a fair number of women played excellent tennis, achieved splendid records and the modest, momentary fame that is the inevitable reward of winning major championships. Indeed, each had, in her own time, notable challengers who were close to being their equals in the matter of talent. But of all the women who have played the game at its top levels, only these two had that sense of style and of self which propelled them from the second-class citizenship to which female champions in all sports shared with men have until now been doomed into the kind of fame that extends far beyond the sport —becoming, as they say, "controversial" figures among people who care nothing about the game itself.

Of the two, it is Mrs. King who may well come to be regarded as the more significant figure when the definitive history of tennis' first century is written. Lenglen shared the world stage with Tilden, after all, and it is possible that Tilden alone could have created the first great wave of popularity for the game, so powerful was his impact on what we now insist on calling the media. King, however, happened along when there was, as previously noted, no male figure on the scene—no Tilden, no Budge, no Kramer, no Gonzales, no Connors—to compel the fascination of the reporters and the cameras, no one to whom the public at large could attach a part of its fantasy life. Nor did there follow in Lenglen's wake a large number of women capable of filling her place when she was finally forced to recede from the center of things. King, on the other hand, fought actively and with enormous skill and guile to secure a permanent place for the woman's game as a central attraction, not a side show, at the great tournaments. She was instrumental in creating a touring circuit that permits women professionals to earn a livelihood equaling that of similarly gifted men. Indeed, as she emerged a whole troupe of supporting players burst through with her: Margaret Court, Rosemary Casals, Evonne Goolagong, Chris Evert, the last of whom, though entirely different in style and personality, will doubtless succeed King as the superstar of this particular drama.

Yet, for all of that, there is something seductively attractive about the older legend, if only because there was always something mysterious, something no contemporary writer or observer could quite get at in the Lenglen story. It seems possible that, as the world's very first woman to achieve world fame beyond the inner circle of her sport, she literally had no models on which to base her behavior. So, for want of something more appropriate, she turned to the world of the stage—with special reference to ballet—for her style, though there was also much of the grand-opera diva about her. One has only to recall the dramatic make-up and costumes she wore when she went on stage, the dressing-room tantrums, the near swoons that came at crucial moments in matches, the miraculous revivals that a slug of brandy could induce when it was proffered in these moments of crisis. One would have hated to play against her, or to officiate one of her matches. But the theatricality of her presence was a wonderful thing, not merely because it was "good for the game," but because it was *sui generis,* and therefore good in itself. And quite unlike anything that has been witnessed before or since on a tennis court.

She was born in Paris (in 1899), but grew up in Nice in the south of France, which was near the home of the Ballet Russe de Monte Carlo, which is said to have greatly influenced not only her balletic style of play (how she did love to leap about the court), but her style of dress. She was the daughter of a cycling champion and he, like Fred Perry a little later, envied what appeared to be the gracious life and expensive accouterments of those he

Story of women's tennis
—which is to say, the dawning
recognition of women as
tennis players—is encompassed
by the years from Suzanne
Lenglen (below) to Billie Jean
King (opening pages). Lenglen brought
a balletic athleticism to
the game, as well as more graceful
dresses and the chic, much-copied
bandeau. King's stubborn
integrity has advanced the cause
of women's professional tennis.

Jack Tar Togs

STYLE · SERVICE
THRIFT

BUSY Miss America chooses *Jack Tar Togs* for work and play. They're so becomingly girlish, so appealing, and at the same time so sensibly serviceable.

Jack Tar Togs are real thrift garments. Their sturdy materials wear and wash perfectly and their well-cut lines hold the swing of style as long as the garments last.

Jack Tar middies, dresses, skirts, bloomers and smocks—the pretty, durable clothes so truly economical to buy and to wear.

You'll find *Jack Tar Togs* in good stores everywhere.

Rub 'em
tub 'em
scrub 'em

—they
come up
smiling.

Look for this label

Write us for *Jack Tar Style Book, Dept. C-1* and give us the name of your dealer.

THE STROUSE-BAER CO., BALTIMORE, MD.

Middie blouse on "Jack Tar"
tennis player of 1919
prefigures the costume of
the youthful Helen Wills, and
the beginning of a
beginning for more comfortable
sports clothes. Tennis
motifs in fashion advertising,
such as belle of 1916 with
flat-topped racket, suggest an
upper-class appeal. Sporty girl
behind spectator sipping Coke
is hobbled by long skirt.

observed playing tennis. It was he who determined that his daughter should excel at this game, and it was he who supervised her training. There are variants in the legend at this point. Some say it was Papa's habit to place a handkerchief at various points on the court and reward Suzanne with five francs whenever she hit it with the serve or shot he decreed that she practice that day. Others say he used to scatter one-franc pieces about the court and allow her to keep those her ball hit. Whatever his coaching technique in this matter, it is certain that the imperative for fitness he had learned as a cyclist was imposed on his daughter, and that this gave her an incalculable advantage in the genteel world of women's, or as it was then known, ladies' tennis. (Despite her rigorous conditioning, the fact remains that Lenglen was not the possessor of a very strong constitution and she died, during the Wimbledon fortnight, when she was only thirty-nine, the victim of pernicious anemia.) As early as 1913, when she was only fourteen, English travellers to the south of France returned home bearing tales of a stunning new presence on the very active circuit of tournaments played along the Côte d'Azur in those days. It was obvious to those who had seen her that she was, despite her youth, entirely ready for Wimbledon. The war, of course, intervened and it was not until 1919 that she made her entrance on the world tennis scene.

But what an entrance it was. What the galleries were used to from women players was very stolid, baseline tennis, though it is true that most of them following the example of Lottie Dod, the first female known to smash and volley (and still the youngest player ever to win at Wimbledon, being just fifteen years, ten months old when she won the first of her five titles in 1887) made occasional forays to the net. Still, it was no easy matter to get there, dressed as they were, and the great women players of the prewar era, players like Mrs. Alfred Sterry (a five-time winner) and Mrs. Lambert Chambers (seven times a victor, and Lenglen's first victim in a championship round at Wimbledon) still appeared on Centre Court dressed as if for a lawn party. And played in that manner, too. The fortnight, for the women players, if one is to believe their reminiscences, was a gay social round, the important punctuation marks in it being provided by teas and champagne suppers—not at all the serious affair it is today, in which, for example, Rod Laver's idea of a big time is to tune in a western on the telly and spend the evening shaving the handles of his rackets down to the fine point that suits him.

Lenglen changed all that. She was not, in 1919, the fashion plate she would be starting the following year, when Patou, the great couturier, would take charge of her costuming, but she did choose a one-piece dress with short sleeves and an accordion-pleated skirt of mid-calf length. No petticoats or corsets for her. "Shocking," "indecent"—these were some of the words used to describe her appearance, for it must be remembered that in those days the ladies' dressing room at Wimbledon still provided an iron bar above a stove on which the players could hang and dry out their corsets, many of which Elizabeth Ryan, the fine American player who holds more Wimbledon titles than anyone else (all in doubles in which she frequently partnered Lenglen), recalled were bloodstained from the wounds their stays inflicted on their wearers in competition.

However, after that first year Lenglen grew still more daring. For example, she was, as far as is known, the first woman to wear make-up on court, in part to cover her bad complexion, but in part, too, because she seemed

to relish her role as a style setter. In 1920, when she took to wearing her short hair wrapped in two yards of silk, the color of which she liked to coordinate with her lipstick, "the Lenglen bandeau" swept not only the world of tennis fashion, but that of the world far, far away from any court. The same was true of her one-piece frocks (which in still later years she took to having run up in silk). To put the matter simply, she was the first woman (and for that matter, the first player of either sex) to place performance above propriety, to dress in a way that enhanced rather than restricted her freedom of movement. And since the beginning of her career coincided with the beginnings of the first stage of women's lib in this century, she became, as King would later, a significant symbolic figure for many of her sex. Not that there was anything inelegant about her. She often wore silk stockings when she played, and frequently draped a fur-trimmed steamer coat over her shoulders on the sidelines.

As for her style of play, it too was a revelation. It was not that she came constantly to net—she actually felt insecure there, some said. It was the wondrous style she employed when she got there that captivated onlookers. There really was a bit of the dance about her leaping overhead and the marvelous extension of her reach for lower-level volleys. Everyone spoke of her remarkable footwork in every part of the court; she seemed never to have to scramble, never to return a ball awkwardly. And, with her loosely strung racket, she exercised remarkable ball control and remarkable patience in long rallies, sending her opponents scuttling back and forth along the baseline until they either made an error or permitted her to move in for the kill.

The legend began to build at that first Wimbledon, when she reached the challenge round against Mrs. Dorothea Lambert Chambers, who was trying for her seventh Wimbledon championship, though very much the underdog on this occasion, given her age (forty-one) and her lack of competition in the tournament. (As the 1914 holder, she had merely to await the end of the competition which was, in effect, to select a challenger for whom-

ever held the title.) She was also evidently the more upset of the finalists when rain forced a day's postponement of their meeting. But when they finally met, with the King and Queen present, on a cool, cloudy, windless day, perfect for tennis, it was she who took the first game and, though she fell behind at 3-1, fought back to extend the first set to eighteen games. At one point in that last game she served, and many in the crowd thought the ball was out, but Lenglen silenced the critics with a gesture and a clear announcement that the serve had been quite good. A few minutes later, she closed out the set with a neat drop volley, which many felt at that point meant the match, since it seemed impossible that the Englishwoman, twice her opponent's age, could come back after such grueling struggle. But Lenglen was perhaps overconfident or—since her reserves of strength were so much less than people knew—overeager to win quickly. She pressed her luck at the net and found herself in difficulty on her serve. Down 4-1, she signaled her father who sailed a flask out of the stands to her. At the time it was said to contain sugar water, though it was later revealed to be a stronger spirit. It did no good and Mrs. Lambert Chambers won the second set 6-4.

Now it looked as if momentum had swung to the defending champion. But Lenglen sprinted off to a 4-1 lead in the deciding set before Mrs. Lambert Chambers rallied behind a service of renewed strength and drew even at 4-4, then broke Lenglen's service to go ahead 5-4, 177 after which she was in her turn broken. But she broke back again and was at 6-5, 40-15—double match point. Now, however, she said later, she started thinking about what the newspapers would say about her remarkable upset—and she lost the game, though not her heart. She and Lenglen exchanged games again, but the sixteenth of them in this set went to the French girl at love and the agony of tension was finally, decisively broken. Lenglen's parents swept her into their arms the minute she had shaken hands with her opponent, and the great career quickly became a study in invincibility. Only once was she defeated in singles competition. That happened at Forest Hills in 1921, the first year the U.S. women's title was contested there. She arrived overconfident and under-trained, and in those days, before draws were seeded, she encountered none other than the defending champion, Molla Mallory, in a match that should certainly have been nothing less than a semifinal encounter. In all, Mallory won the U.S. title four times. She has been described as a human backboard, a woman capable of implacably returning everything that was thrown at her. She took the first set with what seemed to Lenglen humiliating ease, 6-2. Now the Frenchwoman suddenly developed a racking cough, and down 3-0 in the second set declared herself unfit to continue and walked off.

It may be significant that this was the only major tournament at which she appeared unaccompanied by at least one of her parents. It is certainly significant that she never ventured back to the United States, whose climate, if not provably bad for her health, was certainly unhealthy for her reputation.

Elsewhere, however, she was simply unbeatable. In 1925 she lost only five games in winning the last of her Wimbledon titles. A year later she lost only four in winning the last of her three French titles.

This final major tournament victory was sandwiched between the two most significant events of her career: her famous match against Helen Wills at Cannes and her equally famous walkout at Wimbledon. Wills, with her poker face, her eyeshade, and her steely determi-

nation, had begun to build a record of invincibility that was, if anything, superior to Lenglen's. In 1926, she had not yet won Wimbledon (though eventually she would take that title eight of the nine times she played for it), but she had won the U.S. title three times in succession (and would win it seven times all told), and world-wide pressure for a match between these two remarkably dissimilar players was building.

The trouble was that Lenglen would not return to America and Wills was only just beginning to venture forth to Europe. It began to seem that they would never coincide at the same tournament. At which point, enter a former member of the New Zealand cabinet, sometime tennis international, and, more important, the representative of an English sporting-goods manufacturer—F.M.B. Fisher. He and his employers recognized that if their ball were used in the match everyone said could never be played, it would be of inestimable publicity value to them. So the smooth and energetic Fisher began removing the obstacles to the meeting. It was he who found a venue acceptable to both contestants (the Carlton Tennis Club in Cannes), he who found a set of officials both could agree on (Lenglen would permit no

Americans to take these roles). It was he, finally, who orchestrated tennis' first great media bash, the lonely precursor in those nontournament meetings for extraordinary prizes (Riggs-Court, Riggs-King, Connors-Laver, Connors-Newcombe) that have become such a dubious feature of our own age. Doubtless he knew then what we should all know now, that no single meeting between top-level players proves anything, that it is the overall record of their meetings, under tournament pressure, that finally allows one to determine who outranks whom at any given moment. Still, this event suited the spirit of its historical moment as well as those encounters in such odd settings as the Astrodome and Las Vegas seem to suit ours.

Ostensibly no money was at stake, but shrewd John R. Tunis, then one of the world's great tennis writers, later a distinguished writer of sports fiction for youngsters, wrote the classic account of this match, and doing some rough arithmetic based on the price of the tickets, the sale of movie rights, and the known costs of the meeting came to the conclusion that the 300,000-odd francs that flowed into the till must have flowed back out to someone. Tunis hinted darkly that tracing the direction of this "leakage" in the pipes of amateurism "might prove of

much interest to the governing bodies of tennis in England, in the United States, in France." In other words, he imagined the largest under-the-table payoff in the game's history, although, gallant gentleman that he was, there was no possibility of his casting aspersions on anyone's honor—especially women's. One does wonder, nonetheless, just how Lenglen, whose family was not rich, managed to live as well as she did in those days—the life of the diva, after all, not being an inexpensive one.

Still, if she and her opponent did receive rather grander than usual expenses, they earned them, for the conditions at Cannes were atrocious. The Carlton Club, in the shadow of the great and deservedly famous grand hotel from which it took its name, was anything but a grand tennis club. Bounded by four mean streets, it consisted of six clay courts, any three of which at any given moment caught the sun in such a way that one of the players was bound to be blinded by it. The clubhouse was a hut with seventeen lockers (Tunis counted) and a shower that didn't work. One side of the court was bounded by the blank wall of a garage and a sawmill rose above the center court, where its buzzings did nothing to improve the concentration of the competitors. For this historic occasion,

179

Great Confrontation of its day
(l & below) was one-and-only meeting
of Mlle. Lenglen and "Little
Poker Face"—Helen Wills—at
Carlton Tennis Club of Cannes in
1926. Lenglen won 6-3, 8-6,
soon thereafter turned pro, while
Wills went on to dominate women's tennis
for another decade. Opposite:
Lenglen and her fabulous
American partner, Elizabeth Ryan,
who was a doubles winner at
Wimbledon a record twelve times.

bleachers designed to seat some three thousand fans were erected. Indeed, workmen were still hammering away as the players began their warm-up, Lenglen having arrived in style in the Voisin automobile bearing her from the villa she had taken at Nice.

The match itself was more of a struggle than the final score—a straight-set victory for Lenglen indicates—for she was quite rattled by tension of the occasion and by the wretched playing conditions.

Moreover, she found in Wills a mettlesome opponent. The American had, by common consent, the hardest serve in women's tennis up to that time and, perhaps more to the point, she had a temperament that responded extremely well to pressure. She was generally at her best when she was hard pressed or had fallen behind. Lenglen, on the other hand, was upset when she lost so much as the odd game or two in a match, and the loss of a set could bring her to the edge of psychological crisis. In short, the scene as it developed at Cannes in the late morning of February 17, 1926, distinctly favored the American. Canny Frenchmen whose homes overlooked the court sold space in their windows for twenty francs or so, and since many of their roofs featured removable tiles, they sold space in the attics as well. One saw the distinctly odd sight of many heads popping up out of these roofs. Still others found viewing room in trees near the court or on the tops of busses parked in the surrounding roads. Besides that, the crowd, crammed into the inelegant and makeshift stadium (the gentlemen of the press had to support their typewriters in their laps), was unruly, and since the umpire was English and either could not or would not address it in the local language he could not control its noise.

Still, Lenglen got off well enough, winning the first game. She lost the second, however, and that appeared to unnerve her. Even when she moved definitively ahead in the fifth game the cheers of her supporters brought her more pain than pleasure and she struggled through to the sort of victory (6-4) that was, for her, a moral defeat. Her father—bedridden at the time—had

warned her that she was in for more of a struggle than she was used to, and neither her mother's cries from the stand that she should not lose another game to the upstart from California nor the champagne she sipped between sets settled her.

In the tenth game of the second set Lenglen had a match point and Wills' return appeared to her, and to many others, out. She tossed aside the balls she had been carrying and rushed to the net to shake hands with Wills when a linesman belatedly called the ball good. Uproar —and one can but imagine the inner turmoil of Lenglen. But it was she who stilled the crowd and returned gamely to the struggle, losing that game and then trading games until finally, Lenglen took two in a row and the match. One of the Burke brothers, who owned the club, was to say later that at the end of that difficult second set Suzanne "was on the verge of collapse. If she had lost the set she would have been finished."

Still, as she had proved at Wimbledon that first time, she was stronger under pressure than she believed, the ability to come back from a bad call at a key moment being the mark of a true champion. On the other hand, she was, in this same year, due to suffer still greater pressure and to respond very poorly to it.

She was now the undisputed queen of tennis. As noted, she swept grandly through the French nationals, and with Wills out of both that tournament and Wimbledon as a result of an appendectomy, it appeared that nothing could prevent another all-conquering season. No one, however, reckoned with the tennis establishment's capacity for mischief-making. Both her own and the American LTA resented her long-standing doubles partnership with Elizabeth Ryan, and they insisted that each take partners who were also fellow citizens of their respective nations, which was upsetting to both women and caused Lenglen to arrive at Wimbledon in a foul mood. This was not relieved when she discovered that she and her new partner, Didi Vlasto, were scheduled to play her old partner, Ryan, and her new teammate, Mary K. Browne, in the first round. Here, again, was one of those

accidents that the failure to seed the draw inevitably caused. Worse, she had drawn Browne, an excellent player, as her first singles opponent. Worse still, in an exhibition doubles scheduled as a feature of the first day's activities at this Golden Jubilee tournament, she and Ryan were reunited one last time—and were, astoundingly, defeated by a team of virtual unknowns.

It was all enough to unnerve anyone, let alone the high-strung Lenglen. When Browne took five games from her in their opening-round match—it had required a whole tournament's play for Lenglen to lose that many at the previous Wimbledon—she became further distraught.

The next afternoon, late, she and Vlasto were scheduled for their doubles against Ryan and Browne.

And now a riot of conflicting stories mars the narrative. The sequence one can piece together from them is that the Wimbledon committee thoughtlessly scheduled a singles match for Lenglen in the early part of the afternoon. No official informed her of it, although as their star attraction she was used to being taken aside at the end of a day's activities and informed of her schedule for the following day's competition. It was not until late the next morning, just before heading for an appointment with a doctor who was supposed to attend a sore shoulder she had developed that Mlle. Vlasto rang Lenglen to tell her about the singles. That was too much. She was not about to play a singles match, no matter how easy it was supposed to be, before appearing on Centre Court for the featured doubles. She later claimed that she called the referee's office

at Wimbledon to inform his staff that she couldn't possibly play the singles. Unable to get through, she called "Toto" Brugnon, fourth of the Four Musketeers, and asked him to pass the word; he later insisted that he, indeed, had left her message with someone or other at headquarters. It never reached the powers that were, however. They had, meantime, informed the King and Queen that Lenglen, a royal favorite, would be playing both singles and doubles that day. Their majesties took an early lunch, motored down and were dismayed to find nothing happening on Centre Court, except a group of men endlessly rolling and rerolling the grass, stalling for time. At 3:30, in plenty of time for her doubles, Lenglen arrived, was summoned into the presence of the committee and forced to remain standing while they reprimanded her for her carelessness and her affront to royalty. This sent Lenglen howling to the women's dressing room, from which no amount of through-the-door entreaties would budge her.

At last her mixed-doubles partner, Jean Borotra, was persuaded to penetrate that sanctum sanctorum—perhaps the only male who has ever done so during a tournament—and he tried his best to reason with her. She was, however, prostrate. "I can't even stand on my feet," she cried. Borotra, himself, was to later recall he was near the same condition himself— particularly when

the committee members asked him to go to the Queen and explain the situation. *Crise de nerfs*, he told her Majesty, adding "She has it in mind to apologize, but at the moment she is unable to do so. She is very, very sorry."

Caught in the middle, between Wimbledon's committee, on whose good will he, like all players, was dependent, and his friend Lenglen, he did his best to suggest that there was nothing calculated in her affront to the Queen without betraying his disgust at the ineptitude with which the whole matter had been handled. The Queen was gracious and sent her best wishes to Lenglen, while the committee rescheduled her matches for the following days.

When the word went out to the world, however, the press, which did not have access to the inside story, played it cruelly As they had it, the Queen of the Courts, the grand diva of tennis, had at long last gone too far: she had deliberately affronted the Queen of England. The English press, in particular, was vicious in its condemnation of Lenglen and when she appeared next day for her doubles—which she and Vlasto lost, despite twice having match point on Ryan-Browne—the crowds were notably cool. They remained so when she appeared for her singles against a Mrs. Dewhurst, whom she handily defeated. It was not until the mixed doubles, on the

California's Helens locked in battle on Centre Court in 1929 final at Wimbledon. Wills (l) blasted her new challenger, Helen Hull Jacobs, 6-1, 6-2. Note ball passing umpire's head—and fashionable cloche hats in the stands. Straight-set victory was the typical Wills performance In her eight Wimbledon wins, only two players took a set from her in semis or finals.

weekend, where Borotra charmed the crowd with some well-crafted court comedy, that they began to come around.

Still, Lenglen, used to being a darling of the galleries, was severely troubled by the controversy. If, after all, it upsets you to win a set at 6-4, what must it do to you when the whole world is howling about your lack of manners. She brooded over the weekend, then announced her withdrawal from the singles competition; then a little later from the mixed doubles as well. Not long thereafter she said goodbye to all that and turned professional. She never discussed it, but it is possible that she found a certain refreshing freedom from hypocrisy in playing for pay. At least she was free of pompous and self-serving officialdom and, as long as she continued to play, she was an ardent advocate of professionalism. Still, things were never quite the same after she walked out at Wimbledon. Indeed, they still aren't. For all of Billie Jean King's efforts, for all the progress that has been made, women's tennis has yet to produce another star of her unique magnetism—this odd-looking woman with her sallow complexion, outsized nose and crooked teeth that no one noticed when her feet began to dance and her skirt began to swirl on her way to victory.

Her mantle fell to Helen Wills, of course, and if one consults only the record book, not the memories of those who were entranced by the Lenglen spell, it is she who should perhaps be judged the greatest player of all time: eight Wimbledon victories, seven U.S. titles, four French in singles alone, a five-year period from 1927 to 1932 when she never lost a set of singles in competition. As remarkable as anything was the fact that she was still capable of winning at Wimbledon in 1938 (long after she had become Mrs. F. S. Moody), fourteen years after she had first appeared there. Despite her sobriquet, "Little Poker Face" and despite her early predilection for sailor-suit whites, she was a remarkably handsome woman in an austere sort of a way and her game matched her looks. Classic and severe, it featured an extraordinarily powerful serve and formidable groundstrokes, perfectly executed and tirelessly employed. But if her game matched her appearance, it also matched her personality. So far as one can tell, she had almost nothing to do with her opponents off the court and as little as possible to do with press and public. In short, she attracted admiring but not exactly warm audiences, and though, looking back from an age in which "personality" is everything, one must admire her refusal to play to the galleries, one cannot say that she did a great deal to make women's tennis a colorful or very stirring affair.

185

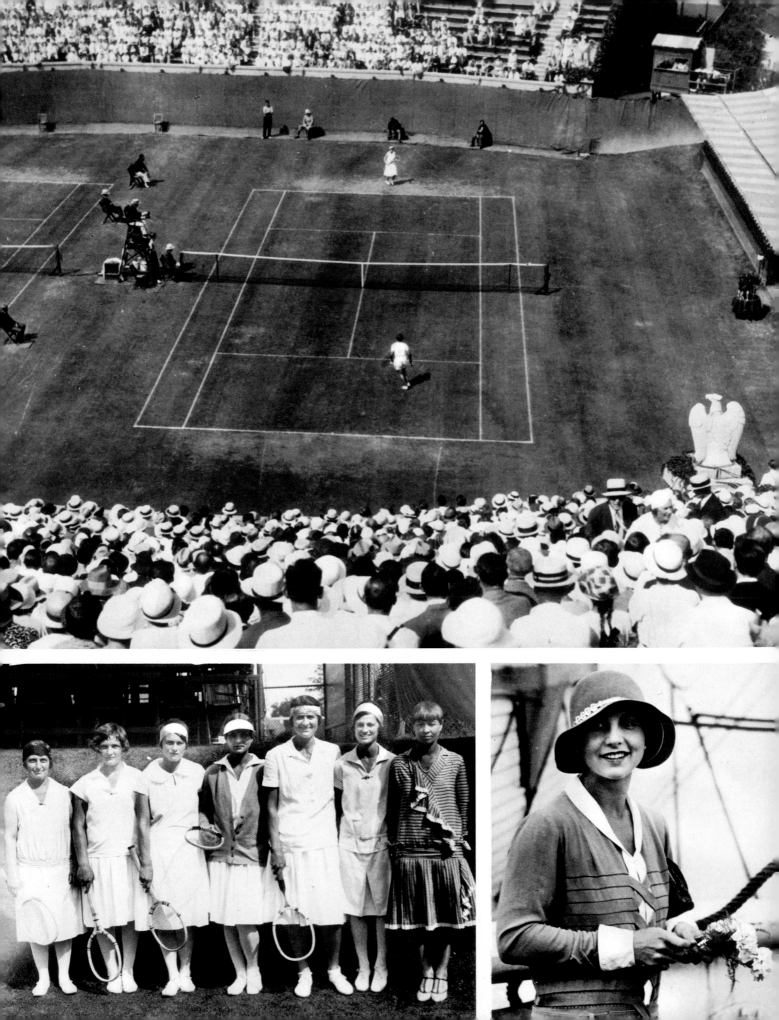

Points in A Career: Helen Wills
with 1927 Wightman Cup team
which defeated British women at Forest
Hills. (Mrs. Wightman and young
Helen Jacobs at l, Molla Mallory at r.)
Smiling return home on **Aquitania**
after some of many victories abroad.
Left: Eighth Wimbledon and
another trouncing for redoubtable
Jacobs, 1938. Above: Sixth
Wimbledon, 1933. Opposite: A rare
loss—to Jacobs in U.S. singles
at Forest Hills in 1933.

187

People took more kindly to the young woman who emerged in 1929-30 as Wills' most persistent challenger. Her name, of course, was Helen Hull Jacobs. Like Wills she had grown up in Berkeley. Indeed, her family at one time moved into the very house the Wills family was vacating there. The book on her was that she had no outstanding shot or skill, only a fierce competitive instinct, "more will to win, more drive and guts than anyone else," as Alice Marble, who came along a little later, put it. Overall, Wills had the edge in their meetings, but by 1933, according to Jacobs, she felt her game had matured sufficiently to beat her arch-rival. Indeed, during practice for the French championships she was drilled on strategy by no less a figure than Lenglen herself, who advised that the only way to beat Wills was with short, sharply angled cross-court shots. Unfortunately, Jacobs got to the finals neither in France nor at Wimbledon. But at Forest Hills, where she was the defending champion, she finally got her chance. And Lenglen's advice paid off. Jacobs won the first set 8-6, lost the second 3-6, and was ahead 3-0 in the final when she turned to see Wills quitting the court, claiming a leg injury had worsened and required her retirement. Jacobs, of course, won the championship —second in a string of four consecutive U.S. titles—but the issue between them was left in doubt. The win could not, in the circumstances, be considered clean-cut. It was two years before they met again in a major championship, this time in the Wimbledon finals, where Jacobs had yet to win and where the crowd was obviously on her side. She was ahead 5-3 in the deciding set, and had match point at 40-30, when Helen Moody threw up a lob that was, apparently, caught in a sudden downdraft. Jacobs went up for an overhead smash and ended on her knees trying to get her racket on the ball. The best she could do was to hit the net cord, the ball bouncing back into her court. She lost the set 7-5.

She returned the following year, and with Wills Moody out of the competition, finally won her one and only Wimbledon title, without, however, changing her luck when it came to playing her fellow Californian.

Two years later she was back on Centre Court, facing Helen Wills Moody in the finals. This time, however, Jacobs was handicapped by a leg injury—a torn sheathing of the Achilles tendon. She played heavily bandaged and was doing well enough (the score was 4-4) in the first set when she went up for another overhead, landed awkwardly, and reinjured the leg. Her ankle started to swell and Hazel Hotchkiss Wightman, donor of the cup that bears her name and is annually contested by teams of women from the U.S. and Britain, came from the stands to urge the umpire to permit a pause to remove the bandage. It did no good and Jacobs lost the set 6-4. Across the net the poker face did not change and now Mrs. Wightman urged Jacobs to retire. But perhaps remembering Wills Moody's retirement for lesser cause at Forest Hills five years previously, Jacobs played on, winning not so much as a single game, but perhaps gaining a moral victory. A day later Bill Tilden encountered her and quotes her as saying about Wills Moody: "You know, Bill, I don't mind her being a so-and-so, but I object to her being a stupid so-and-so. If she had only smiled when she shook hands at the end and said, 'I'm glad you broke your damn leg'—or something like that. . . ." True to form, however, Helen Wills Moody won her last Wimbledon as she had her first, without outward display of any sort. Except for the lapse reported by Tilden, Jacobs has always stoutly insisted that there was never any feud between them, that their relationship was always pleasant, if not cordial. But her protestations strike one as pro forma, the sort of thing you would expect from a woman who played by the Aussie creed before there was an Aussie creed.

Jacobs just never gave up. As early as 1936 she had lost her U.S. title to Alice Marble who, before turning pro in 1940—perhaps prematurely—successfully defended it four out of five times, the last two against Helen Jacobs, who kept hanging in there against the new dominant player just as she had against the old one. Marble was a wonderfully aggressive player with perhaps the finest volley anyone had seen in women's tennis until that time. Had she not turned pro, it seems likely that she

189

Left: Ball compresses on
racket of Althea Gibson, on her way
to winning second-straight Wimbledon in
1958. Her reign was short,
however, as she decided to capitalize
on success and turn pro.
Right: Margaret Smith—now Court—
was a physically powerful
Australian who used the same
training methods as Aussie men, and
battled the lissome Maria
Bueno of Brazil for pre-eminence
among women players of 1960s.

might have continued as the leading player of the war and postwar years. Certainly there was no one as strong among the group which traded the major titles among themselves for the rest of the decade: Pauline Betz, Louise Brough, Margaret Osborne duPont.

Maureen Connolly—"Little Mo"— was, however, a different story. A true prodigy, she was only sixteen when she won her first U.S. title in 1951, seventeen when she won Wimbledon on her first attempt, and nineteen when she became the first woman to win the Grand Slam (1953). A sunny girl, with a stunning backhand, she was essentially a baseliner. With her sweet face wrinkled in fierce concentration that was almost comical, she was a crowd-pleaser who might well have advanced the woman's game greatly in popularity had her career not been cut short by a horseback-riding accident.

Again, the sinewy Althea Gibson, the first black to break the color line in tennis, might have led women's tennis to greater heights of box-office appeal, as she, too, combined pleasant temperament and a strong game. The color barrier (as well as a certain lack of ferocity) slowed her development, and when she finally came on strong, winning Wimbledon and Forest Hills two years in succession (1957 and '58), she felt she had to cash in quickly on her hard-won success. She turned professional,

however, at a point when it was immeasurably harder for women to succeed, considering that it was backbreaking for a man to make a decent living.

In the early sixties it was essentially Margaret Smith (better known now by her married name, Margaret Court) and Maria Bueno who were the leading players. Court was a rather too placid stork of a girl, possessed of enormous physical strength and undeniably the first truly great Australian woman player. Bueno was a small, aloof, fluid-stroking Brazilian, whose graceful movements found favor with the crowds.

It is almost impossible to choose between their records between 1959 and 1965. Court won Wimbledon in 1963 and '65, while Bueno won it in 1959, '60, and '64. Court won at Forest Hills in '62 and '65, while Bueno took the U.S. title in '59, '63, and '64. This slight edge by the Brazilian, whose game depended on delicate timing that could go off and who was, as well, plagued by injuries, was offset by the fact that Court won French titles in '62 and '64, a championship Bueno never won, and by Court's remarkable record of seven consecutive Australian titles, 1960-66. With the smaller, frailer Bueno lacking the stamina to continue heavy campaigning in the late sixties, it appeared, as writer Grace Lichtenstein has said, that Court had but to stand around and await her coronation

191

as the unquestioned ruler of women's tennis. She reckoned, however, without a feisty youngster named Billie Jean Moffitt, who is now, of course, Billie Jean King.

She started turning up at Wimbledon in 1961, where she was put out in the first round. The next year she drew a bye in the first round, Court in the second and beat her, the first time in the history of the tournament that its number-one seed had been defeated in her opening match. Court got her revenge in the next two years, defeating King in the finals in '64, the semis in '65. Then, in 1966 King made it to the finals against Bueno, having lobbed Court to death in the semis. She took her first set in the finals by using the same tactics, lost the second as Bueno put away overhead after overhead, then settled down to playing grim, controlled tennis. She rushed Bueno out of the match, losing only one game in the third set. King now had her first championship. She retained it for two years before losing it to Ann Haydon Jones and failing to regain it in 1970, when she lost to Court as the Australian was duplicating Maureen Connolly's Grand Slam.

King's record continued to be somewhat patchy over the years. She won Forest Hills, for example, in 1967, but did not regain that title until 1971 and '72. She won in Australia in '68, but lost the championship to Court the following year, and won the French title only once (1972) in a period when Court was taking that championship three more times.

Major titles, however, are not the entire story here, for Court's problem is that she is, like so many of the Australian men (though for different reasons), media-proof. Perhaps because she is such a large woman and so singularly strong (she is a believer in the strenuous gym and road work that have served her male countrymen so well), she seems to have a compulsion to prove that she is more of a lady than anyone else. She also lacks court smarts, the ability to vary her game, to outthink an opponent under pressure. This has led to the widespread belief that she chokes, does an "el foldo" (King's phrase) in important matches. And surely both failings were painfully evident in her infamous loss to Bobby Riggs in their

Ms. King's racket flies
high during well played and
fondly remembered final against
Maria Bueno at Wimbledon
in 1966, for first of three
straight triumphs there.
Below: Olga Morozova,
25, of USSR, is a player
of promise. She made Wimbledon
and French finals in 1974
(defeating King en
route in former), but lost both
to inexorable Ms. Evert.

Evonne Goolagong of Australia
is blithe, elegant, and immensely
popular with tennis crowds.
She serves brilliantly, moves
about the court with elfin
grace, and first won prominence
with Wimbledon victory
in 1971, when she was 19,
beating King and Court en route.
Following year she lost
to Billie Jean (below), who
is holding her head in pleasure
after tempestuous finale.

infamous exhibition match in 1973.

None of these criticisms applies to King. "Pressure—I love it. I don't know why. Why do you rise to an occasion? Pressure. It spurs you on. I feel the adrenalin flowing." If Court's career, so like Lenglen's in this respect, can be read as an attempt to avoid pressure, to get in front and stay in front, King's can be seen as an attempt to seek out trouble and crowd-pleasing drama, to keep things hot for herself, which is doubtless why she has involved herself in so many off-court challenges, has said and done so many things that could only turn galleries, and the tennis establishment, against her. It gives her an extra incentive to prove herself now, in a time when she has nothing left to prove as a tennis player. It keeps her restless intelligence busy, gives it something more exciting than an old tennis ball to chew on.

Other than the famous victory over Bobby Riggs in the circus atmosphere of the Houston Astrodome in September, 1973, there are very few classically memorable matches in her record. She speaks fondly of that first Wimbledon win over Bueno; of her semifinal win over Chris Evert on the way to her 1971 victory at Forest Hills, halting a streak of Evert upsets that had won the public's heart. And she relishes the greatest single shot she ever made: a cross-court backhand on match point in the Wimbledon finals against Evonne Goolagong in 1972—not the safe, percentage shot, but a wonderfully daring and imaginative point that she brought off so perfectly it still apparently gives her gooseflesh just to think about it (and makes her one with all the duffers of the world who treasure similar moments of isolated perfection against the long summers of discontent).

But it is not the isolated match or tournament that makes her, as she likes to put it, "Numero Uno," it's her whole life that brings her satisfaction, that has made her a force to be reckoned with in the history of the game. It's odd, but to the outsider she strikes one as very like the man she beat in that orgy of hype in Houston, Bobby Riggs, the difference between them being that she found socially useful outlets for her questing intelligence, while

Below: King gave Bobby Riggs
a good trouncing in television match
at Houston Astrodome in 1973.
In carnival atmosphere, she avenged
Court's earlier defeat by Riggs
and asserted dignity and competence
of women players. Feisty,
intelligent, and interested in
life outside parochial
world of tennis, she finds her
leadership challenged by ruthlessly
accurate game — and unassailable
youth — of Chrissie Evert (r).

**THE
VIRGINIA SLIMS
CIRCUIT**

You've come
a long way, baby.

King (opposite) has fought loudly and hard for parity with men in split-up of tournament prizes. She is not alone in women's struggle for recognition, but she has willingly, generously committed her considerable prestige to the cause (including such ventures as Slims tour), and at some risk to relations with tennis establishment. Rosemary Casals (below) has been active pro since 1968.

he did not.

She is very like him in background—an unwealthy kid up off the public courts of California, snubbed by the establishment for violating their dress codes and their belief that young players should not speak unless spoken to, yet full of ambition and not immune to the charms of, say, the Wimbledon fortnight—such a correct and classy affair. She was like him, too, in her insistence on playing her own game, which was rather a contrary sort of thing stylistically. He played, in effect, a woman's game on the men's circuit, while she played a man's game on the woman's circuit—a hammering, hard-charging affair. Where she was lucky was that she came along when tennis was ripe for a change. He was caught up in an historical moment when there was not only no chance for change but also, during the war years, hardly any tennis to be played when he was at the top of his form.

What seems to have shocked her into liberationist action was the discontinuity between her feeling of accomplishment when she won Wimbledon and the world's merely mild interest in her feat. "Nobody gave a shit," she said. She turned pro, along with three other women and sampled the hard and psychically unrewarding life of those tours to nowhere. She welcomed open tennis and then found another discontinuity—this time between the rewards offered women and those offered men. This issue has been obscured by a good deal of blather since, but what King claimed was not that women were equally as competent as their male counterparts, but that their contribution to the financial success of the typical tournament was, and that they were entitled to something like equal remuneration—that being the way of things in show biz, which, she kept reminding everyone, big-time sports are, at least in part.

The issue came to a head in 1970, when Jack Kramer, who promotes the Pacific Southwest tournament in Los Angeles, was recruiting players for it at Forest Hills. First-place money for the winner of the men's tournament was to be $12,500. The total prize pool for women was $7,500. And this was in a context in which, while the WCT

offered a profitable tour for the men, the USLTA offered a thing of rags and patches for the women pros—little money and less continuity. Led by King, who was sitting out Forest Hills, the women talked of boycott while attempting to reason with Kramer. Both efforts came to naught. Whereupon Gladys Heldman, editor of *World Tennis*, stepped into the breach, offering to stage an alternative invitational tournament for women in Houston in competition with the Pacific Southwest. The USLTA refused to sanction it, which meant that anyone who played in it would probably be banned from its events for a while. Mrs. Heldman then offered to make every member of her draw a contract professional for the week, the truce then in force between the USLTA and the pros being that players under contract to any recognized promoter were free to come and go as they pleased in LTA sanctioned events. The ploy was transparent, the LTA threatened banishment, but the women played anyway, then extended their contracts for six months and, partially supported by a cigarette concern, launched their own tournament tour.

King does not take credit for the creative pragmatism that went into the invention of this tour, but it was her presence on it as the ranking star that made it possible, and it was her tireless advocacy of it that made it a success and, evidently, rejuvenated her interest in the game. It put her in a position to make the Riggs match the great hustle that it was, and it put her in a position to front for the dubious notion of team tennis, as well as the excellent idea of publishing a sports magazine for women. It even motivated her on the court. When she won at Forest Hills in 1971 (defeating Goolagong in the finals after her semifinal win over Evert), she felt she was playing for the honor of the Virginia Slims tour (neither of her last opponents was a tour member). When she won at Forest Hills in 1974 she felt she was playing as a representative of World Team Tennis, which many traditionalists were erroneously convinced would have a ruinous effect on individual ability, ignoring what she has chosen to ignore as well—its ruinous effect on the balanced structure of the game itself.

How to sum her up? Basically, I suppose, as a woman who has broken through the stuffy conventions of behavior which were infinitely more onerous in women's tennis than in men's; as a player who derived enormous—and openly expressed—pleasure from the game and the rewards which success in it brought her, but who insisted that there was more to the game, more to life, than could or should be contained in the sports pages. And, contrary to the grim image often presented of her in those pages a mercurial, but essentially likable and, above all, effervescent personality. A dialogue with Grace Lichtenstein, the writer, sums up that last point. After a couple decades of endlessly hitting a tennis ball, did she, could she, still get any pleasure out of it, the reporter asked.

"It's music," King cried. "It's dancing. Sometimes I sing to myself to get a rhythm. . . . To hit a ball right, when you're on the balls of your feet, your body's working the way you want . . . it's the greatest thing in the whole wide world."

"Does anything else give you that much pleasure?" Lichtenstein asked.

"Sex," she shrieked. "Don't print that."

But one is, of course, glad she said it and glad the remark was printed. We have, indeed, come a long way from those corsets drying on the bar in the locker room at Wimbledon. And there is some irony in the fact that it is in this stodgiest, most tradition-bound of games, that women athletes have made their most significant advances, that the example of their free spiritedness and candor has led to a general loosening of attitudes among the men as well. One also likes to think that perhaps Lenglen, whose free spirit lacked a way of expressing itself, was driven inward on itself in a somewhat neurotic fashion, would have approved. King has made a glorious fuss, and one looks forward to the day when the women's draw at any major tournament will be filled with strong players who have come to the game as a result of her example—and who have perpetuated her spontaneity, as well as her skill.

forest hills: the twelve-day week

Forest Hills, or at least that portion of it where the West Side Tennis Club is located, has the slightly out-of-kilter look of the typical American compromise with other cultures—in this case a vision of an English village in something like Tudor times. One can imagine its attractions when it was set down in the semirural reaches of Queens early in this century, before Megalopolis engulfed it. Offering the middle-class citizen solidity and comfort, it touched these virtues with a hint of the exotic, the distinctive, as well. One can see why, when the tennis club decided to move from crowded, expensive Manhattan in 1913, the setting struck the members' fancy. They were, after all, devoted to an English game that could, despite its comparatively recent origins as an outdoor sport, trace its antecedents at least as far as the local architecture could trace its stylistic influences.

In August, 1974, I felt as I had before when invading these environs, that I was entering a region where time, though it had not stopped, had certainly congealed. What I was interested in discovering, after an absence of many years, was how much time had seemed to speed up in the small world that has taken root in this small world—the U.S. Open Tennis tournament, successor since 1968 to the closed, amateurs-only, national tournament for which, in the old days, it had generally been possible to buy a ticket—even for the final day—simply by strolling up to the ticket window a few minutes before the matches began. That, I knew, was now impossible, and I wanted to discover, by spending all day every day at the tournament, what else had become impossible now that tennis had become a big-time, big money sport.

Inevitably, little changes have occurred with the passage of the years. The castle-like hotel which dominates the cool, leafy town square no longer takes in transients, and its restaurant has been converted to a brew-and-burger franchise. The darling little shops, complete with leaded windows in some cases, are mostly deserted, the commercial action having flowed a few blocks north, toward bustling, characterless Queens Boulevard. But the residential sections surrounding the old square (through which one must approach the tennis club) remain as well kept as ever, and every few feet signs warn intruders from the outside world of dire consequences should they leave their automobiles against these law-abiding curbs for any appreciable length of time. Happily, these injunctions are not enforced when the U.S. open is in progress, but one gets the idea: Forest Hills, like its tennis club, which by playing host to this tournament since 1915 has made the town world-famous, feels embattled, slightly paranoid perhaps, about the way things keep changing, the way the world keeps intruding on what was once a well-ordered, parochial way of living.

The grounds of the club, as they are dressed for the big event, have an antique patina. The flags of many nations fly from the top of the half-century old, very well-designed stadium (I never found a really bad seat in it, except in the press box located in the marquee at its open end). Around it many tents are clustered, creating at first glance the impression that one has stumbled into an old-world bazaar or folk festival.

Such romantic fancies quickly disappear as one passes through the gates. The tents, it turns out, are mostly for the use of various corporate enterprises whose promotional "tie-ins" with the tournament include not only the right to flash messages from the electronic scoreboard in the stadium (I'll never forget that 4711 was the "official" cologne of the 1974 U.S. Open), but the right to stage boozy lunches for clients under these canvases.

Indeed, almost everywhere you turn at the tournament, your eye is assaulted by some form of huckstering. Each and every court has an ice chest, bearing the strange device "Pepsi-Cola" and well-stocked with same. God help the player—Arthur Ashe, for example—who has a tie-in with a rival soft drink (Coke in his case), or who in mid-match develops a craving for some other refreshment. (In 1973, Stan Smith decided that all that stood between him and victory was a shot of Gatorade and despatched his fiancée, Marj Gengler, for that magic elixir. None was to be found anywhere on the grounds, its manufacturer not having contributed to the prize-money pool, and Ms. Gengler

Opening pages & below:
The stadium at Forest Hills
is a product of the
Tilden-inspired tennis
boom of the 1920s.
Eating facilities, rest
rooms, press accommodations
are primitive, the grass
was strictly alas (and has now
been dispensed with). But there
is not a really bad seat in
the house, and it can handle
a respectable 15,000.

Stan Smith (l) arrives
carrying, besides his several
rackets, a troubled
serve and a faltering
confidence. The 1971 winner,
he fell to Roscoe Tanner
in the quarters. Arthur Ashe
(opposite), 1968 champ,
was hoping for one of his
hot streaks, but also
survived only to
the quarterfinals.

had to run all the way to Waldbaum's supermarket on
Queens Boulevard to obtain it.) It is a bazaar all right, but a
very modern, hard-nosed, charmless sort of a bazaar.

Once the crowd begins to arrive one is quickly
disabused of even the more modest fantasy that perhaps a
note of fashionable elegance, something reminiscent of the
teens or twenties of this century, will be struck here. To be
sure, an elderly traditionalist or two will turn out in a blue
blazer and club tie—and coats and ties are required of
umpires and linesmen—but for the most part the crowd is
tacky in a way that would distress an habitué of Wimbledon. Dress is strictly Central-Park-in-a-heat wave, manners
subway-in-a-rush-hour. This is the democratization of tennis in full, weedy flower.

The opening rounds, in particular, are a night-
mare. For in addition to the stadium court and two courts in
the smaller, wooden grandstand near that great concrete
edifice (quite the nicest place to watch tennis on these
grounds, by the way, since the permanent stands are
shaded by fine old trees), seventeen other field courts must
be used in the early going to accommodate all the matches
required to reduce the huge player population to manage-
able proportions. For a great national tournament is actually a congeries of several tournaments: men's and
women's singles and doubles, mixed doubles, senior men's
singles and doubles, junior tournaments for boys and girls
and, in this case, something called the Grand Masters,

Searching out a unique vantage
point is a Forest Hills tradition.
Little boys specialize in sneaking peeks
under the wind-screens, while
treed photographers also
are common sights. Booths under the
stadium sell not only rackets and togs,
but all the latest gadgetry alleged
to work a magical transformation in the
hacker's game. The commercialism is
choking, but necessary if the prize pool
($271,720 in 1974) is to be
rich enough for major-tourney status.

which brings together older players who in previous years won, or at least were capable of winning, national tournaments. This means that some very good tennis, often involving seeded players, more often pitting well-matched competitors of the second flight, are in constant progress on the field courts. Narrow walkways separate these courts and there is a constant push and shove as spectators move from match to match, sampling the wares on display (again the bazaar analogy occurs), looking for upsets in the making or a match that has reached its moment of decision. Their attention span is very much that of the age of television (i.e., short), and the constant movement and chatter from the sidelines must be one of the most difficult tests to which a player can submit his powers of concentration.

Nonetheless, until the men's singles field was reduced to approximately the round of sixteen, it was the field and grandstand courts I haunted. The theory was simple: Almost any tournament is going to be won by one of the top eight seeds. (The only unseeded player ever to win Forest Hills was Fred Stolle in 1966, and no unseeded player has ever won Wimbledon.) So there is plenty of time to see Connors or Newcombe or whoever among the favorites strikes your fancy. Indeed, most of them turn up at one time or another in the outlying precincts during the early days of play. Meantime, there is a great deal of attractive tennis being played in circumstances about as intimate as you'll find at your own club. If, for instance, you want to get a sense of what it is like to face Roscoe Tanner's famously powerful serve, the place to do so is when he is playing on a grandstand or field court. It is also a place to discover the human virtues (and the technical skills) of players who don't make many headlines. Out here, in the early going, one finds underdogs to root for.

Such a one, for me, was Mark Cox of Britain, whose chief claim to fame is that he was the first amateur to defeat a professional—Gonzales no less—at the world's first open tournament at Bournemouth in 1968. On the first day at Forest Hills he was playing young Jeff Austin of Rolling Hills, Michigan, on the number-four court, hard by the stadium. Cox has curly blond hair, chunky legs, and the

dogged courage we like to think characteristic of the English. At thirty-one he was feeling the sultry heat much more acutely than his younger, fleeter opponent, who has the look of an intense chipmunk, a tendency to foot fault, and a habit of talking to himself in a not altogether engaging manner.

Cox got off well, with 6-3, 7-6 victories in the first sets, then began to fade in the heat, losing 3-6, 1-6. He won my heart during this discouraging patch when he looked up at us railbirds during a changeover and inquired pleasantly, "Anyone want to stand in for a set?" He was to say later that part of his trouble was an inability to decide what to do once he had gained his two-set advantage: go for a quick kill in the third set or pace himself for a longer match. He compromised, neither going quite all out nor finding it in himself to totally tank the two sets, in the process permitting the momentum to pass to Austin. Now, in the final set he rallied and found himself—after an exchange of service breaks—involved in a tie-breaker. Worse, he was down three match points in it. By this time, however, Austin's second serve was weakening and Cox began pouncing on it, at last bringing the match to a single point. He had the serve, followed it in, and made one of the best shots of the tournament, a cross-court volley of tremendous daring. Austin may have had a chance at it, but he also saw that it was heading perilously close to the sideline and decided to leave the decision in the lap of the gods. The ball landed in by inches and Cox dropped to his knees to salaam to those gods.

Afterwards, as I walked with him to the clubhouse, he had to reject autograph seekers because his hand was shaking too hard to hold a pen. "To win when you're down three match points," he cried in high excitement. "What are the odds on that? A million to one?" I asked him what had been going through his mind during the tie-breaker. Mainly, it turned out, that the only time he had ever played Austin before, both sets had gone to tie-breakers and that he, Cox, had won them both. If he remembered that, he reasoned, so did Austin, and that had to give Cox an edge. And what about that daring cross-court

volley that ended the match? "I had a choice on that shot, where to aim, but I remembered making it against Ken Rosewall here a couple seasons ago. I remember thinking, 'Maybe it's a good shot for Forest Hills.'" Professional tennis players talk that way. They remember—their muscles remember—what ours do not. Like the rich, they *are* different from you and me, and I learned in brief exchanges like this one to resist tempting analogies between their game and ours.

At the time it seemed to me that Cox was too intelligent to spend his thirties as early-round cannon fodder for better players, also too nice a guy to ignore as he tried to move through this tournament. I watched him in an easy five-set win over Jiri Hrebec of Czechoslovakia in the next round, and a tough loss to the extraordinarily graceful and attractive Alex Metreveli of Russia in the third round. This was another five setter, featuring three tie-breakers and eliciting from Tom Okker, sitting near me in the grandstand press section, an admiring "good stuff" as he reluctantly rose to leave for his own match while the issue was still in doubt. Since then, however, I have been pleased that Cox, after being used as Rod Laver's sparring partner in preparation for the $100,000 match against Jimmy Connors (Cox is left-handed, like Connors), went on a wonderful tear, winning three out of four WCT tournaments and proving himself capable of unsuspected heights.

Roscoe Tanner, another unseeded player, was beginning to prove the same thing right here and now. Indeed, he probably should have been seeded, because he has, by common consent, one of the six or eight best serves in the world and is thus a man to reckon with on grass. Unfortunately, on clay and other softer surfaces he has not done well, and so his overall record is not so impressive to tournament committees as it should be. Nor was his first-round victory over tiny Mike Estep, a Czech transplanted to Dallas, terribly impressive. That serve is Tanner's best weapon and it was not yet working at full efficiency.

Still, he lost only one set and, ironically, gained confidence from his performance, feeling that if he could win even when his serve was inconsistent, it was a good augury for the rest of the tournament, when he was sure it would return to full power. Today he was content to throw up a lot of lobs, partly because Estep is short, partly because he had lately played a lot of team tennis. "When I first come outdoors," he said, "those lobs look different as they come out of a clear sky."

For his part, Estep kept a cheery face in adversity. "Oh, he's so smart," he cried, when Tanner outdueled him at the net at one point. A little later he watched one of Tanner's amazing aces blaze past him and turned to the small gallery, shrugged, and said, "I just refuse to go for those."

By the end of the match, I had decided that Tanner was a man to keep an eye on. In part this was because in the last set he got his serve working and it struck me as perhaps the biggest one I had ever seen. In part it was because he was young and strong, and perhaps on the brink of seeing his game peak. I could imagine him sneaking quietly through a section of the draw that was not fraught with power and going a long way.

Meantime, there were Stan Smith and Arthur Ashe to worry about. They were the only Americans—other than Connors—among the top eight seeds, and since one of the subtexts of this tournament was the powerful desire of players and spectators alike to see the gauche Connors and his then-fiancée, Chris Evert, denied a repeat of their "love bird" double victory at Wimbledon earlier in the summer, it seemed only right to develop some sort of rooting interest in those of their countrymen who seemed to stand the best chance against them.

Neither had enjoyed especially good seasons. Smith had been co-ranked number one with Connors at the end of the previous year's competition, despite the fact that Connors had beaten him in the majority of their confrontations and had been outspoken in his insistence that Smith owed his ranking more to his ability to go along with, get along with, the tennis establishment than to his current skill with the racket. There was probably some truth in this, because Smith is nice to the point of blandness, while Connors is abrasive to the point that players as varied in temperament as Ashe, Laver, and Okker have publicly been critical of him. There was no disputing the fact that as they came into Forest Hills, Connors was the better player, having won the Australian and English titles, as well as just about everything else he had set his hand to. (Had he not been barred from the French open as the result of one of his many disputes with the power elite, he would almost surely have been working on a Grand Slam.) Smith, on the other hand, had won nothing of note and was having trouble with his serve, which is at once big and delicate, since he hits the ball not at the apex of his toss but precisely at the moment it drops six inches from that point—which means that small errors in timing can throw him off more than they do other players. Everyone was hoping he would start a comeback at Forest Hills.

As for Ashe, who is an excellent money player on the WCT circuit, but who has only a couple of major titles to his credit, he was saying that he thought this might be his last chance to win the U.S. title for a second time. He is aging, of course, but he is also a serve-and-volley player, which means he likes to play on grass. Since, after years of complaint about the turf, the West Side Tennis Club had finally decided to get rid of its grass after this tournament, Ashe felt that the slower surface of future years would further diminish his chances of winning.

Grass, and what might replace it, was indeed almost as powerful a concern in this tournament as the assault on the Connors-Evert axis. Since the press rarely ventures out of its air-conditioned lair in the stadium, and therefore has very little to ask the players when it confronts them in post-match conferences, the newsmen were absolutely bewitched by the subject. There was universal agreement that the grass was, as usual at Forest Hills, terrible, but there was a lively controversy over what ought to replace it. The professionals, in meeting assembled, recommended what they believe to be the fastest of the new composition surfaces, Plexi-pave, but the club finally opted for clay, the surface least beloved by American and Australian pros. Partly, one suspected, this was the club's way of getting back at them for all the years they had bitched about the Forest Hills grass. Partly, one imagined, class considerations entered into the decision. Concrete, asphalt, and variants thereof are public-court surfaces. Clay, which is not inexpensive to keep up, is very much a private-club—and eastern seaboard—surface.

Be that as it may, none of the people in whom I had developed an interest had an easy time of it in this tournament. Smith, for instance, drew the excellent Jaime Fillol of Chile as his first-round opponent, got tied up in a players' meeting in Manhattan, then in traffic on the way to the tournament. He arrived rattled and in lively fear that he might have to default. As a result he lost his first set to Fillol. Then, just as he started to settle down in the second set, rain settled down over Forest Hills and, since it was late in the day, play was suspended. The next day Smith closed out the set, but could not break Fillol in the next set and was himself broken in the twelfth game to lose 5-7.

I was sitting in the grandstand press section as it happened, next to Marj Gengler, who spent a good deal of the match covering her eyes and uttering fretful remarks. ("If he loses his serve now, I'll brain him.") She advised me that she is "not as bad as Sharon Lutz [wife of Smith's doubles partner, Bob Lutz]. "She throws up—and she cries when Bob loses." The next set is scarcely easier for Smith, though his serve has stiffened sufficiently so that he can advance confidently behind it, and his overheads are really crackling. Even so, he fails to capitalize on a service break at 4-3, being broken back immediately at 4-4, which means he has to go to a tie-breaker just to stay alive in the first round.

This brings a lemming-like rush from the press box to the grandstand. Number-three seeds are rarely threatened in the first round of a tournament. Marj is putting a brave face on the situation: "His pattern is that when he struggles in the early rounds he does well in the tournament." Still, she cannot bring herself to watch when Smith, leading 4-2 in the tie-breaker, serves for the match. It is a very good serve—perhaps his best of the day—and Fillol is not at all sure but what it might have missed the service line. However, linesman, umpire, and Alan King, comedian

The two veterans, Smith
(l) and Ashe (below)
were overshadowed by young
Roscoe Tanner (opposite),
who advanced to a
semifinal confrontation
with Connors behind
an awesomely swift and
powerful serve. When his
groundstrokes and tactical
sense catch up, he will
challenge Jimmy (among others)
even more strongly.

Another Comer: Bjorn Borg
arrived riding a hot
streak (victories in the
French and Italian Opens) and
closely followed by
teen-age fans who treated
him like a rock star.
Fourth seeded, he was put out
in the second round by
India's Vijay Amritraj in
four sets. Only 18,
Borg obviously had many
years of winning ahead.

and tennis fanatic, who had positioned himself along the fence that separates grandstand from court, all call it in. I have to tell Marj that her betrothed has won, and as we depart King is still showing anyone who is interested the exact point at which Smith's serve kicked up chalk.

Things will now ease off a bit for Smith, whose wins over Frew McMillan, Brian Teacher, and Sid Ball in succeeding rounds will all be comfortable, but never, perhaps, so overpowering as they would have been a year or two earlier. He keeps telling people that, after all, this has not been "that bad a year," that the difference between it and an exceptional one comes down to a few key points that might have gone either way. Yet he is playing cautiously, tentatively, even as he slides through these early rounds. His aura is that of a man who can be had.

The same cannot be said of Ashe. They say of him what they say of Smith; that he spreads himself too thin, plays too much, has too many outside interests, although some of them are inevitable for the only black man playing world-class tennis. They also say he is streaky and, maybe, too gifted for his own good. His repertory of strokes is as extensive as that of anyone in the game, which means that he can, for example, choose between eight subtle variants on a backhand return of serve, which gives him too much to think about at moments when you would prefer instinct to take over.

In any event, he has an easy first-round match, and then a tough second-round match against Vitas Gerulaitis, a young player who, just a few months later, would begin to hit the first peak of his career. Even worse, the match is scheduled on the so-called clubhouse courts. These are the oldest patches of grass on the grounds —though in no better shape for the length of their history—and some players refuse to accept scheduling there. The problem is that the membership of the West Side Club foregathers on the terrace, glasses clinking in hand, gossip very much in mind, and they set up a frightful din. Club members are by no means universally in favor of the employment of their turf as a venue for the national championships—all those vulgar strangers tramping

about—though the event contributes so much to their coffers that dues are lower than at any comparable club in the nation. Therefore, there is some pressure on the tournament's managers to stage at least a few choice matches near the sacred veranda, so the membership (which is admitted free to the tournament) can watch without bestirring themselves.

This is Ashe's second match here and his encounter with Gerulaitis can be regarded as typical of the worst that players have to contend with in the opening rounds at Forest Hills. The players appear on court at their appointed hour to find—unbelievably—no officials, no ball boys, not even a can of balls to employ in a warm-up hit. After a while someone on the second-floor veranda—it is reached from the men's locker room—tosses down a can of balls so they can at least begin their hit. As they do, a child asks in a clear, piping voice, "Mommy, which one is the American?" Of course, both players are, and, indeed, Gerulaitis is a member of the West Side club. Mom, however, declares with complete confidence, "Mr. Ashe, sweetheart." The kid studies the black man for a moment and with equal confidence declares, "He doesn't look American," which perhaps says something about the progress of social awareness in a club that achieved a certain notoriety by denying a member of Ralph Bunche's family access to its courts two decades ago. "Well," the woman replies, "he's the most famous."

That vignette concluded, officialdom begins arriving on court. The match gets underway with one line judge missing. In due course he arrives—and strolls casually behind Ashe just as he is preparing to serve. Ashe glares, the umpire scolds, and, unbelievably, the man takes his seat at the midpoint of the sideline—where he could not call any imaginable shot in or out. Ashe sets down ball and racket, walks over to the man, exchanges a few words with him, and then moves the chair to its proper position —where the man can see if a ball landing near the baseline is in or out. Ashe then proceeds to the ad court for his next serve, only to perceive that an ancient LTA pensioner is sitting in the wrong position to call the service line to which

A Study in Contrasts: Evonne
Goolagong (l) demonstrates the serene
manner that generally accompanies
her fluid shot-making. Below:
Some of her competitors prove that
ferocity is not an exclusively
male prerogative. Clockwise are
Virginia Wade, who won Forest Hills
in 1968; Chris Evert, who has yet
to win anything here but the gallery's
heart; Julie Heldman, unseeded
but a semifinalist, and Rosie Casals,
who lost in the quarters.

Ashe will be addressing himself. Another halt, another rearrangement of the furniture by the tournament's number-eight seed. His work for the day is not yet finished, however, for yet a third official has drawn his chair up to the court as if it were a fire from which, despite the sweltering heat, he sought to draw warmth. In this position, of course, he may well interfere with play, and once again Ashe takes it upon himself to station the official properly. All of this Ashe performs with what one has come to think of as the modern American black man's customary manner: dignified patience covering, but not entirely disguising, disgust.

The first two sets are close, 7-6, 7-5, but then Ashe closes out quickly, 6-2, and moves on into the third round, where thirteen of the tournament's sixteen seeds are still alive. Only Tom Gorman, a merry and graceful man, has gone out in the first round, and Bjorn Borg, the teen-age idol, and Manuel Orantes have failed in the second.

Like Smith, Ashe will struggle through to the quarterfinals, and like Smith he will be pressed, but never with great firmness. After his easy third-round win over Australia's Geoff Masters he is asked if each new victory helps build confidence, and he snaps, "Well, my confidence is better than Geoff Masters' right now—and that's about all." Which indicates that his self-esteem is not in quite the sieve-like condition of Smith's, but that the question of its strength is very much on his mind. Things are just not quite right with him. "I can't seem to fall back and regroup," he admits at one point.

Indeed, of the players I have chosen to follow closely in this early going, only Tanner seems actually to be growing in wisdom and in valor before my eyes. In his second-round match with Britain's Roger Taylor he drops the first two sets, though he seems to start grooving his serve late in the second set, and takes the next three sets with the kind of easily growing confidence that an older player would give anything to enjoy. At one point, I look up to see that Pancho Segura, Connors' coach, has joined the small gallery around the field court and I hear him say to a companion as Tanner whistles one of his aces past Taylor, "Jesus Christ, remember when you could do that?" He

notes, as Tanner himself does in later interviews, that the effectiveness of this weapon derives in part from his low toss, which means the extraordinarily hard-hit ball skims the net at an extremely flat angle. The ball is thus harder for the receiver to track and it is likely to take a low bounce, too, when it hits the playing surface. It is an admirably unpretentious serve, and one does not imagine Tanner will ever have the trouble with it that Smith has with his more fussy stroke.

On the other hand, as Segura informs us, this weapon is so much the most powerful at Tanner's command that he tends to rely on it too heavily, which could put him at a psychological disadvantage in certain tight situations. Suppose, for example, under the pressure of a tie-breaker his nerve briefly falters; what does he have to fall back on?

Watching Taylor trying to contend with Tanner's heavy hitting (his groundstrokes and volleys are brutes, too), Segura says, "If he's smart, he lob on heem"—in other words counterpunch. One then remembers that Segura is no idle spectator. He is Jimmy Connors' coach and he is present to scout a potential opponent. In time, one will see just how valuable this canny old pair of eyes is to Connors.

For me, at this point, Connors and the number-two seed, John Newcombe, might as well be playing in another tournament. It is simply impossible to take in everything that's going on in this huge sprawl of action. For example, the women, especially in the early rounds, are just simply not so interesting to watch as the men. Catching a glimpse of their matches here and there one begins to sympathize with the male players' opposition to prize parity with them. Their draw is half the size of the men's draw, meaning the winner has to play one less match than the male winner. But that's not where the real difference lies. The fact is that with Olga Morozova out of this tournament, and with Martina Navratilova not yet at the peak she achieved the following winter on the tour, there are only five or six good players on hand: King, Evert, Goolagong, maybe Casals, and Julie Heldman, who is having an exceptionally good tournament while Virginia Wade is having an exceptionally poor one. The result is a lot of boring tennis, many lopsided matches. The women's tournament, unlike the men's, does not really get interesting until the semifinal round.

As for events in the men's doubles and the mixed doubles, one can only afford to give them glancing attention, though perhaps the pleasantest experience of the tournament, for me, came late one afternoon as twilight fell on the nearly deserted grandstand court where Billie Jean and her longtime partner, Owen Davidson, were playing Estep and Navratilova in a second-round match. It was a surprisingly tough match for King-Davidson. (They were seeded first, but did not win the title, which went to Geoff Masters and Pam Teeguarden.) Players do not take the "mixed" entirely seriously, and more than anything else I witnessed at Forest Hills there was about this encounter the air of a weekend match of the sort you and I are likely to find ourselves in. There was a lot more chatter back and forth across the net and between partners, much of it taking the form of mock anger. What developed was a sense of shared peril among all four contestants. They quickly discovered that they were all playing against the man in the umpire's chair, who persistently announced the wrong score and seemed, several times, to have nodded off up there on his perch. (The shortage of officials, especially of competent ones, is one of the minor scandals of the tournament, and since big money is now riding on their decisions something really ought to be done about it; perhaps they ought to be paid something more than an honorarium and a free lunch each day they work.) Anyway, this was a good match—King and Davidson pulling it out after losing the first set in the tie-breaker—loose and very human, in large part because chirpy little Estep was not intimidated by King. He was perfectly willing to engage her in chin-to-chin arguments across the net over disputed points, positively eager to test her by playing to her power. It was, one must imagine, a way of releasing tournament tensions, of having some fun in the midst of a scene that cannot offer the players much of that quality. Watching the match, I felt I had been allowed

to witness a privileged, private moment.

Meantime, my little tournament was beginning to flow into the larger tournament—the tournament people were reading about in the papers and would shortly start seeing on national television. In the third round Tanner surprised the seventh-seeded Ilie Nastase, coming back from a two-set deficit to do so, squeaked by El Shafei to enter the quarters against Smith. We were in the stadium now, where it is impossible to determine the psychological flow of a match as you can in the grandstand or out in the field. But it seemed to me that when Tanner took the first set on a tie-breaker the match was, in effect, all over. Roscoe took the next set 6-2, relented to give Smith a set at 3-6, then crushed him 6-1 to move into the semifinals.

Ashe, too, was doing pretty well. Drawing Guillermo Vilas in the fourth round, he knew he was coming in against a good young player who was riding a winning streak. In a tentative mood, he lost the first set on a tie-breaker, largely because he was being too cautious with his first serve. His return of service was never so authoritative as it might have been, and his volleying seemed to me to lack the crispness I had observed in it elsewhere. (Of course, he is notorious for his lack of faith in his backhand volley, a matter he talks about, according to the other players, almost obsessively.) Still, he had one of his strong streaks going for him in the second and third sets, and despite doing a sort of walkabout in the fourth set, he was able to break Vilas with both forehand and backhand passing shots in the twelfth game to take the deciding set without resort to a tie-breaker. Later he told Vilas that "your serve got shorter and shorter as the match went on," that that was the major weakness he found to exploit.

So now he, too, was in the quarters, facing Newcombe in a premier match that was, for some reason, scheduled for the grandstand court (which Newcombe humorously imagined Raul Ramirez must have commandeered for a midnight bullfight, so bad was the surface). Needless to say, this was the kind of confrontation that draws a crowd and it could not be contained in the stands. It flowed out on to the grass of the unused second court and

222

Inside Story: Lounge
outside men's locker room
buzzes with gossip and
deal-making, resounds with
the slap of cards, the
constant click of
backgammon games, which
help players like Jimmy
Connors keep their minds off
forthcoming encounters. In
dressing room, comedian-tennis
fanatic Alan King
does some hanging out.

there was a certain raffishness about the atmosphere, in part because the spectators sprawled on the grass, so close to the court, felt less constrained than they would have sitting densely packed and upright in the hard wooden stands, in part because a lot of blacks turned out to cheer Ashe on. He is, as always, his cool, correct self on court, but his fans, though amiable and loose, feel free to urge him on in terms that are distinctly not approved by the USLTA. "Man, hustle. You gotta hustle for those," one youth shouts as Arthur chooses to conserve resources instead of pursuing a difficult get. "Hey Art. Just one more. Just one more, Babe," someone else cries as Arthur delivers an ace while fighting to hold serve. On the whole, it is hard to imagine a better match than this one. Newcombe, to be sure, wins, but in five of the toughest sets imaginable: 4-6, 6-3, 3-6, 7-6, 6-4. There was no "turning point" in the match. Ashe was in it right up to the final point, playing solid, yet imaginative tennis, as steady in his way as Newk was in his—nothing streaky or flaky about him today.

This was my first long look at Newcombe and, wearing his pink "lucky" shirt, he is a charmer. Yes, there is a wonderful ferocity about his game, but it is tempered by what I can only describe as a kind of existential humor, a great white-toothed grin flashing beneath his Keystone Kop mustache as, after a rally, one of his desperation shots dribbles along the net cord and falls in for a winner, and he invites his opponent to join him in appreciating the absurdity of such a fine point being decided by pure chance. Similarly, when luck runs against him, he seems to find

consoling humor in the notion that cosmic issues are decided by sheer luck.

So it is to be Newcombe against Rosewall in one semifinal, Tanner against Connors in the other, and my impression is that neither match is likely to be the walkover for the favorites that many seem to be predicting. Aside from Ashe and a hammering four-setter against his doubles partner Tony Roche, who is getting his game back after successfully submitting his crippled tennis elbow to a faith healer he found in the Philippines, Newcombe has not really been challenged in this tournament, while Rosewall, whom I have been sneaking off to watch whenever I could, has had a succession of tough tests to pass. Charlie Pasarell, Raul Ramirez, and Vijay Amritraj have all extended him to four tough sets, and though he never looked flustered, he did give the impression of a man grateful for challenging practice rounds. "I wish he'd get old," Newcombe said before the match, and by the time it was over he had every reason to wish it even more.

Newcombe started off serving beautifully and had he kept it up, he would have blown his fellow citizen from Sydney off the court. Somehow, however, he seemed to lose confidence in the serve toward the end of the first set, got tangled up in a tie-breaker which he won, but which seemed to hearten Rosewall, who in any event seems to like to use the first set as an opportunity to study his opponent. He is glad to win it, of course, but not sorry to lose it, and in this instance he seemed to sense that Newcombe's serve was not so domineering as it can be and he began working

224

his guileful way to net behind his canny returns of serve and took the next three sets with—considering the round and his opponent—remarkable ease. Yet another of these sets went to a tie-breaker, and this time Rosewall won it and received a standing ovation. One could not quite believe one's eyes, and one had the feeling that Newcombe shared that feeling, that at some point in the match he became a sort of spectator at his own defeat, entranced in some way by the miracle to which he was both witness and victim. In any event, he was a befuddled and angry man when he left the court. Just hours later, he and Tony Roche managed to get themselves knocked out of the doubles competition, mostly because Newcombe was too down to care.

Now it was Connors' turn. I had watched him play only intermittently through the week, but I had attended a number of his press conferences and observed him in locker room and clubhouse, and had begun to feel an odd sort of pity for him. All athletes of championship caliber are, perforce, single-minded, which is another way of saying that they are narrow-minded, in their pursuit of excellence. Most, however, trouble to learn—or recall—a few modest graces to ease them through their inevitably trying encounters with press and public and, since those are somewhat less difficult to master than the intricacies of, say, a drop shot, they do well enough. Connors, I noted, was trying very hard to catch on to these tricks, but he was simply terrible at it. His compliments to his defeated opponents always struck a false note, his little flurries of humor generally fell flat. Like everyone else around the tourna-

Newk and His Nemesis:
Awaiting Ken Rosewall's serve
(l) in their semifinal
match in which Newcombe was
stunningly upset. Below:
Rosewall demonstrates his sure
backhand touch, while
Connors characteristically
engages in some sort
of interplay with the crowd.
Uncharacteristically,
on this occasion it appears
to be semi-light-hearted.

227

Rain descends to complicate
the already intense scheduling of
a high-pressure tournament.
From top: Referee Mike Blanchard
suspends semi between
Evert (facing camera) and Goolagong
midway in second set. Chris
confers with Jimmy.
King is less than enthusiastic.
Evert and Goolagong count
raindrops from shelter of marquee.
Two days later, clouds roll by,
play resumes, Goolagong wins.

ment I spent a good deal of time wondering what was wrong with him.

There are, of course, reasonable explanations for his isolation from the rest of the tennis world. These revolve largely around his choice of a mentor, who is a man named Bill Riordan. He is convinced that there is an informal conspiracy between ILTF, the WCT and the ATP (the touring pros' union) to exercise monopolistic control over world-class tennis. (Davis Cup competition is ruled by these groups, which is why his boy won't play in it.) Considering the quite violent conflicts and uneasy peace among these entities, this seems nonsensical. What one can say for certain is that for reasons impossible for an outsider to sort out, they have pretty much locked Riordan out, leaving him to run a small-time tournament tour, the chief— indeed, only— attraction of which is Connors. The latter claims that he is not legally bound to Riordan, that he can play anywhere, anytime he wants to. It is merely that he doesn't want to play as often as the WCT requires its players to do. And, of course, he is justifiably angry that the ILTF banned him from the French championships in the summer of '74, costing him his shot at the Grand Slam, merely because he had played team tennis, the schedules of which conflict with the ILTF's spring schedule of European tournaments.

These, however, are justifications for Connors' isolation, not explanations of it. And one searches in vain through his brief biography for the sources of his attraction to the role of rebel without a discernable cause. His mother and grandmother—both strong players at the regional level in their day—taught him the rudiments of the game and found him an apt and eager pupil. Tennis was all he wanted to do and it is perhaps revealing that even as a child he claims he "never had time for friends or anything else. I didn't even *know* anybody in school. I was too busy. I used to leave class every day at noon to practice tennis." There he developed the greatest of his skills, his magnificent return of serve, by working out on the hardwood floor of an armory, which was faster than any surface a player is likely to encounter anywhere on the tour. It forced him to challenge every serve early, sweep it back before it could spin away

from him. Still, he did not do remarkably well in national junior competitions. Finally, the Connors ladies moved with him to Los Angeles, where Segura—with a little help from Gonzales—took over his training, working particularly on his serve and volley, but making no dent in his crustaceous personality. He was a hungry player, but hungry only for wins, not popularity. And the former started coming his way in the early seventies. It may be —though this is the purest speculation—that Segura, who never won any major titles and who, with his comic Ecuadorian accent, may have been something of an odd man out in big-time tennis, saw in Connors an instrument for revenging past hurts and slights. Or not—who can say?

The important thing is that Connors has had, so far as an outsider can tell, a good, interesting, rewarding twenty-three seasons on earth. There is no visible wound that would account for the paranoid cloud that seems to hover over him, not even a history of the kind of adversity that, say, Gonzales had to overcome en route to his status as a legend. Can it be that it is only the ineptitude of inexperience that so puts one off him, that he will outgrow all this?

I don't know. What I did observe in the Connors entourage was a distinct air of "us against them" and a singular absence of anyone to instruct him in the gentle art of public relations. All he really had going for him was a steadily growing reputation as a punishing tennis player, a reputation that had begun to build when he quit college in 1971, having observed that if he had been a professional instead of an amateur he could have earned some $50,000 for the performances he had turned in that year in tournaments. For a couple of seasons thereafter he had lurked around the fringes of the game, ambushing this and that star in this and that tournament, but never getting further than the quarterfinals of any great national tournament.

Then, in the summer of '73 he won the National Professional title at Longwood and the Pacific Southwest, and things started coming together for him. He won the Grand Prix Masters tournament in December. (It is said that the very correct Stan Smith had tears in his eyes when Connors beat him in an earlier tournament, and it is a

matter of record that Smith did not wait to walk off court with him, as tradition dictates, when Connors beat him in the Grand Masters.) He won the Australian title a month later. And after being banned from the French championships he swept through Wimbledon, crushing Rosewall in the final—which didn't add to Connors' popularity. Now he was the number-one seed, the man to beat, at Forest Hills. And still, seemingly, no one liked him. The galleries remained essentially hostile, the press difficult, his fellow players unaffectionately respectful. When he was not busy controlling his anger or trying lamely to ingratiate himself, Connors seemed honestly befuddled by the fact that all his victories had failed to win the hearts and minds of the tennis community.

Now as he appeared in the stadium with Tanner (their rackets borne by lovelies wearing tennis frocks fashioned of Kodel, "the fabric of American life," as the public-address announcer informed us to a smattering of bored boos), it finally came over me who Connors reminded me of: Richard M. Nixon.

By that I mean to say that he is a narrowly ambitious man, concentrating a furious energy on a narrowly defined goal—being a winner in his chosen field. To this end, he will sacrifice anything—the graceful presentation of self, the pursuit of pleasure whether it be cultural or merely idle, warming human relations. It accounts for that air of dark suspicion that hangs about him, his powerful feeling that everyone is out to make a fool of him. It is not necessarily so, but the fact is that he has no guile, no wit capable of turning attacks on him back on his attackers.

And there is irony in this, for that is the very basis of his style on court. "His counter shots, returns, and passes are what beat people," Jack Kramer has said. "Longer rallies, more all-court, more lobs, and he runs around a lot." Quite literally, he steals his opponents' power and turns it against them. And he was to give a superb example of that in his match against Tanner. It may be, as Connors was to say later, that Tanner was tired from a succession of tough matches by the time he and Connors met. It may also be that Roscoe disobeyed tennis' basic

dictum, which is not to change a winning game. For it seemed to me, at least in the early going, that he was not serving as hard to Connors as he had to the other men he had met, that in effect he came out trying to throw change-ups at him. But that was a bad tactic, for Connors, besides being able to handle serves the rest of us can't even see, does have this dogged capacity to reach any ball and straighten out—with sheer power—any spin or slice. Then, too, Connors was throwing up a larger number of lobs than was customary, even for him, and I recalled Segura's courtside scouting report, indicating that Tanner was vulnerable to this shot, to soft stuff of all kinds for that matter. (It seemed to me Connors was employing the touch volley more than the usual amount, too.)

Now, on the scoreboard the first two sets could not have been closer, 7-6, 7-6, with both players losing their serves twice in each set, but the first tie-breaker went easily to Connors (what a wonderful weapon a fine return of serve is in this situation), and the next one went even more quickly to him 5-2. Again one recalled Segura's remark that a big serve can be a detriment in a tie-breaker if its possessor has nothing else to fall back on. Connors then ran out the match at 6-4 in the next set, having achieved psychological dominance through those tie-break victories. And, one must add, through his relentlessness. This was the first of his matches I had sat through from start to finish and it is that quality, finally, which seems to me to distinguish him from everyone else. There just doesn't seem to be any way to wear him down, discourage him. He runs for everything and he gets shots that no one else now playing the game does—not with his consistency, anyway.

So it was to be Wimbledon all over again in the finals—Connors vs. Rosewall. The only consolation for the determined Connors haters was that his fiancée, Chris Evert, had been put out in the semifinals by Evonne Goolagong. Play in that match had begun under threatening skies on the final Friday of the tournament and Ms. Goolagong, who likes grass, had whipped Chrissie, who does not, 6-0. She was leading in the second set 4-3 (and up a service break) when the rains came and play was sus-

231

A King and Her Court: Billie Jean cuddles her trophy and makes her fourth Forest Hills victory speech. At right behind her is tournament director and former star, Billy Talbert. From far left: King backhand, King back-of-the-hand (she's putting an official in his place), and King forehand. Left: Finals opponent Goolagong tries to cope with all that. Following pages: Jimmy Connors at the top of his winning form.

pended. It was the sort of luck that Evert seems to attract. (Lesley Hunt had had her on the ropes at Wimbledon earlier in the summer when rain forced suspension and gave Evert a chance to regroup and win.) And, indeed, after another day's suspension for wet grounds she came back to win the second set 7-6.

Standing at the baseline, awaiting serve, there is something oddly complacent in her posture, her weight more on her heels than most players, looking somehow more demure than anyone else. And she plays like a ball machine—mechanically hitting the lines with her instruction-book groundstrokes. When she misses, you don't feel that she has made a mistake. You feel the attendant has just slightly missed the proper setting on her control dial.

In the end, Evert cannot tame the delightful Goolagong. To borrow a phrase, Evonne floats like a butterfly and stings like a bee, and she is surely the most graceful player in women's tennis, combining a nicely tempered ferocity with a sweetness of spirit that communicates itself to the furthest reaches of the stadium. She came back to win the final set of the Evert match 6-3. It turned out that Evert was able to hold service only three times in the entire match.

This victory puts me in some conflict as the finals begin. Goolagong has won my heart, but Billie Jean is the kind of person I've liked ever since Howard Hawks started making women like her the heroines of his movies: intelligent, straight-talking, asking no quarter and giving none in male company, and all the more attractive for being endowed with these allegedly "masculine" traits. In my mind anyway, the line from Katharine Hepburn, Rosalind Russell, Jean Arthur and Lauren Bacall to "the old lady," as Ms. King now refers to herself, is entirely clear. One night as I was leaving the grounds she was walking down the road ahead of me, escorted by one of the male players. He said something that amused her, and the terror of the tennis world, the possessor of the fastest lip on the circuit, suddenly broke into a merry, girlish soft-shoe dance. Nice.

I tried, for awhile, to preserve my neutrality in the King-Goolagong final. Evonne won the first set 6-3, then lost the second by the same score. She was up 3-0 in the deciding set, when King put on one of those gutty rallies that make her such an exciting performer. She broke Evonne's serve, was herself broken, then broke back again and again, finally taking the set and match 7-5. Somewhere in that run I started pulling hard for her. She is not, after all, getting any younger, but more to the point it is clear that tennis alone does not present enough of a challenge to her busy mind, that probably this would be the last Forest Hills at which she would be a fully committed contender.

The women's final, in any case, was a satisfying match and it salved some of the hurt one shared with Rosewall over his humiliation by Connors, who beat him 6-1, 6-0, 6-1 just before the women took the court. About this match, the less said the better. Connors made Rosewall look old and the rest of us feel old, in administering the worst defeat ever inflicted on anyone in this tournament. Rosewall won only nineteen points serving in a match that was over in just sixty-nine minutes, also a local record. What can one say? Rosewall's game simply matches as badly as anyone's can with Connors'. Normally, of course, Rosewall compensates for his serve's lack of power with clever placement, but Connors' ability to retrieve anything anywhere on the court nullifies that skill, and his power on the return of serve is so shocking that Rosewall could simply not get the net away from him. One should not have to point it out at this late date, but for the record, Rosewall is not so bad a player as this score indicates. While we are at it, though, it should be firmly noted that Connors is as good a player as this score demonstrates.

It was that fact that the press was grappling with in the post-match conference. They were trying at last to reconcile the fact that an unpleasant, or at least difficult, personality had somehow been joined with an indisputable talent. Once again, the Nixon analogy recurred, for he, too, had won most resoundingly at a moment when the leading edge of the culture, the opinion-makers, had decreed that his type, the inhumanly ambitious, win-at-any-cost public figure was done in America, when a sweeter image was deemed a prerequisite for any success.

Heavy stuff for the conclusion of a tennis tournament. And I was glad to put it out of my mind as, with a few others, I sought out Rosewall, that composed and sedate figure. A few desultory questions were put to him, but the purpose of the exercise, I think, was simply to gather consolingly about him, to suggest, wordlessly as it turned out, a sense of gratitude toward him and solidarity with him. Indeed, by this time, I had developed a powerful fellow feeling for quite a few of the personalities who had emerged from this twelve-day week. I thought back on the numerous Amritraj family, dark-complected Indians, the women dressed in saris, moving en masse through the crowds to watch one of their three sons play a match, as sweetly prideful as the family of a high-school valedictorian. I thought of Virginia Wade, whose feet kept getting into inextricable tangles in her second-round loss to Ann Kiyomura, and the burning anger that kept bursting through her English reserve—oh, Virginia, how often I've been there. I thought of a spectator standing next to me, and his startled, pleased exclamation when Roscoe Tanner blew an easy drop volley. "It's worth the price of admission to see one of these guys pull something like that," he said. I thought of Stan Smith trying to hide the pain of his struggle with himself and his out-of-kilter game, layering blandness over

the shocking suddenness of his descent from number-one ranking. I flashed, finally, on a twilight scene after the semifinals. I was standing on the second-floor veranda of the clubhouse when my eye fell on a lone figure trudging across the now-deserted field courts. It was Roscoe Tanner, just defeated by Connors, taking the long, but crowdless way home—a small, lonely figure, alone with his mistakes, but, I hoped, consoled by the distance he had come from the unseeded pack to the semis. Beneath the commercial fandango, the media orgy, the human essence of the game as a naked confrontation of will and skill seemed to me very much intact, and here at the end I find myself as unwilling to say goodbye to this scene, to the people who had permitted me to share a little of their experience. as I have been, in the past, to leave an especially splendid cruise ship or to take my leave of the people with whom I had shared the camaraderie of making a film.

Finally, though, there were no more excuses to linger. The moment with Rosewall passed and it was time to go. But as we headed up toward the clubhouse along a path that borders the Har-tru courts that ring the grounds, we noticed a small crowd had collected. What to our wondering eyes should appear but Ilie Nastase and Vitas Gerulaitis, long-gone from competition, but in need of a tune-up for an upcoming tournament in New Jersey. They were not having a hit, they were having a match and they were going at it hammer and tongs, playing fierce and wonderful tennis (despite his reputation as a troublemaker, Nastase is an enormously graceful player and in many respects a pleasant fellow, capable of a wit as genuine as his buddy Connors' is false). They finished a point as Nastase, retrieving the ball, glanced up to see the gallery they had attracted. "Is all over," he said. "Why don't you go home and watch television? You have good television here." Doubtless it seems so to a Rumanian, and in any case we should by this time have been tennised out. Still there was something so pure about this action that we edged away from it slowly, returning reluctantly to the world where tennis occurs on weekends, and the things Nastase and the others do routinely are, for us, miracles.

237

"only connect"

He was very old—in his eighties, I'm certain—his rounded but not soft body balanced precariously atop skinny old legs that were experiencing the utmost difficulty supporting him as he changed from street clothes to tennis togs. It was impossible to imagine them carrying him about the court. Yet here he was in the locker room of the West Side Tennis Club on the first Sunday of the U.S. open—an incongruous spectacle among the lithe, fit young men dressing for the tournament. Having glanced his way I went about my business.

Twenty minutes later I passed him again and observed that he had made but little progress in suiting up for his game. I also observed the cause of his delay. His old eyes had comically deceived him and he had managed to get his jock on backwards, an error he was now slowly, painfully, but quite unembarrassedly attempting to rectify, as one or two club members drifted by to exchange words of greeting with him—a process greatly complicated by the fact that the old gentleman had removed his hearing aid while changing and had not yet reinstalled it.

There was something almost noble about the old guy. There must have been 20,000 people on the grounds that day and though, manifestly, few of them would be paying much attention to games proceeding on the courts reserved for club members, it was also true that many thousands of them would be passing by, and I noticed that these courts were not overcrowded during the tournament, for who among us wants to put our game on contrasting display when the professionals are out in force. Yet Herb —for that was the name I heard him called by—was obviously in the habit of having his tennis game of a Sunday afternoon. It was, doubtless, the anchor of his week—just didn't feel right about things if he didn't get it in—and saw no reason to change his ways just because a lot of damned strangers had taken it into their heads to go tramping around his club, his turf.

A little later, idling along in search of a Pepsi, I got my chance to see Herb in action, though that is not perhaps quite the word I want. He was playing mixed doubles with his wife against another couple only slightly younger. The speed was strictly slow motion, something like that tennis game without balls and rackets in *Blow-Up*. Except that Herb and friends could in no sense be regarded as parodying the game. Their strokes were almost childishly slow, but they were uncannily accurate and mercilessly sadistic in their placement, dropping gently into spots all over the court where ancient legs could not hope to reach them. One could almost hear the sound of inner cackling as the old codgers made their put-aways.

It is true that Herb, even with the battery pack of his hearing aid tucked into a special pocket on his tennis shirt, had some difficulty hearing the score as one or the other of the women—who seemed to be in charge of that matter—called it out, but their match was being contested as seriously, as intently, as any on the grounds that day. Indeed, there was something very moving about it—the utter absorption of the players in their game, their brave refusal to accept the notion that tennis is necessarily a youthful pleasure. I thought of all the old people I knew who had bowed to someone else's definition of what was and was not suitable recreation—some doctor or clucking in-law—and admired these people for insisting on setting their own terms in this matter.

And I thought, too, of the power this game exerts on those of us in its thrall, the power to overcome, in this case, the inertia that age imposes on everyone, the seductiveness of narrowing one's world to this chair, that TV set and a cranky inwardness in which the world outside the door is perceived only as a threat.

Somehow, that match set me to thinking about the strangest one I had ever gotten involved in. My wife and I had gone to an island in the Caribbean to recuperate from New York for a few days, and discovered that though the tennis court at the resort where we were staying was in excellent condition it was, perhaps, unique in the world for being under utilized. There was only one doubles team available for competition: a young, single woman who, until we arrived, had been playing singles against the black man who was the maître d' in the club's excellent restaurant. He was much the best player among us, but that was

240

Their costumes were passing strange. One fellow had no laces for his sneakers and their tongues lolled out of them like those of dogs suffering from the heat. Another had cut a pair of white work pants to tennis shorts length. Yet a third was playing in a knitted Tam O'Shanter and mirrored sun glasses—very disconcerting, for when you played the net opposite him his eyes never betrayed his intentions regarding the next volley.

I cannot say that their initial response to our presence was entirely cordial. This, after all, was by common consent their territory. Sylvanus, however, had a few quiet words with them, apparently assuring them that our passion for the game was equal to theirs and that we were, at least within the boundaries of the court, brothers and sisters under the skin. And so it proved to be. They were good, but we were not so bad; thus we could understand, share, the anguish of the easy shot fluffed, the momentary triumph of the difficult shot made.

And so we played the afternoon away, changing partners at every set. A heavyset man who had hurt his hand and was playing less than the rest of us umpired most of the games, calling out scores and making line calls with just the faintest satirical edge to his impersonation of white officialdom.

Sitting out sets, chatting with others on the sidelines, I discovered that they had learned the game largely by watching visitors play at the resorts where they worked as waiters and such-like during the tourist season. They had also picked up invaluable hints, in recent years, by watching matches on television, the signals of the stations in Miami just barely reaching their island. Their rackets were those which visitors had abandoned or presented to them as tips. Balls, I gathered, were ferreted out of the underbrush near resort courts.

A tropical storm finally cut short our play, but before we broke for the shelter of our cars there was a solemn moment when we all stood at the net, rain drenching us, to shake hands and exchange compliments on each other's games. I believe we all thought it had been, in one way or another, a highly instructive afternoon. I have

all right—we could give them a game and, indeed, we gave them many for several days, until the owner of the resort took up residence and forbade us to play with Sylvanus. Didn't look right to have the help playing with the guests. We found this extremely irritating, since Sylvanus had the afternoon off on Sunday and we had it in mind, the four of us, to play our brains out for as many hours as we could stand.

No problem, said Sylvanus, if we didn't mind taking a little trip by car. There was this other court. . . . So off we went, bucketing up a series of narrow back roads until, suddenly, we emerged on a headland overlooking the sea where, miraculously, a tennis court stood in splendid isolation. The fence around it was deteriorating, but the court surface, very hard and slick, was in better condition than the one we had been playing on, seemed, indeed, to have been freshly painted. The facility, it turned out, had belonged to another resort that had gone bankrupt and it had been appropriated by the island's blacks, four of whom were engaged in a furious doubles match when we appeared.

"It is . . . why we play
no matter what inconveniences
the world imposes on us,
what defects of
physique or temperament
we carry on to the court.
We seek here what
we seek everywhere — a
moment of grace in
a graceless world. And
we find more of
them here than we do
anywhere else."

played in a lot of places: on a movie director's private court (the studio's bonus for a huge box-office hit) and in the town square of a small New Hampshire town, at a fashionable country club and in a backyard in Westport, on the cracked clay of Randall's Island under the Triborough Bridge in New York and on a bubble-covered pier jutting into the East River, not far from Wall Street. But this game, in this unexpected place with these unexpected partners, taught me that the universality of tennis' appeal had scarcely been tapped, that what we are now experiencing as a boom in the game may someday seem like hard times, a pioneer era.

Some of the reasons for this are obvious. A tennis racket still costs less than a set of golf clubs and you can lay down probably a hundred tennis courts for what it costs to create a golf course—and still consume less space than that peculiar sport requires in a world where space is becoming a rare commodity. Then, too, as I said at the outset, there is a seeming simplicity to the game that is very seductive. It hooks you by looking easy (as well as aesthetically satisfying) and only slowly reveals its devilish demands —by which time you are likely to be hopelessly entrapped in a passion from which only death offers honorable release. But there is more to the matter than this.

The other day I was watching the Masters' golf tournament on television and it was, by any standards, an excellently suspenseful entertainment, with three fine players in contention for the title right up until the final hole. But since I was in the process of writing this book I was less interested in the outcome than in trying to penetrate the mystery of this odd game's appeal, especially as it contrasted to that of tennis, with which it so often finds itself linked in argument. I admired the concentration the three leaders (Jack Nicklaus, Tom Weiskopf, and Johnny Miller) were able to muster under the enormous pressure of this prestigious event, the (to me) exotic skills they were employing. But, as on the few occasions when I have attempted the game, it struck me as a mad enterprise.

To begin with, it is such a damnably approximate sport. Even these great players can only roughly instruct the ball as to which of the literally infinite number of

243

flight paths they would like it to pursue and they cannot —try as they will—even make it avoid the most obvious, visible hazards: bunker, trap, pond. Beyond that, they have no control whatever over its final bounce. I mean, it may land precisely in the target area, but who can say where its final roll will take it, what nearly invisible declivity it will discover, what boggy patch it will find?

These matters, obviously, are the province of God or chance—different words for the same thing. But since neither is by nature malevolent the sane man cannot curse them for long. But who else is there on whom or on which you can lay off blame? In other sports—tennis among them—you can place at least part of it on your opponent. And you can revenge yourself upon him, or at least have a

good time trying.

In golf, however, the poor fellow is likely to be a hundred and more yards away and preoccupied with his own problems. So you must take the entire responsibility for your failures on yourself, leading to bouts of introspection unimaginable in any other activity that is supposed to give one pleasure. I truly don't know how they stand it, these golfers, piling this load of guilt and self-loathing and self-pity on those already overloaded carts they have to wheel so awkwardly around with them.

The game, in short, strikes me as the perfect expression of another, older society, a sternly individualistic, and essentially unsociable society—the society described in *The Lonely Crowd*, which not uncoincidentally was the key volume of social commentary in the period when golf achieved its greatest growth in the United States. What David Riesman and his associates described there, you will recall, is a world in which men were essentially alienated from their work and from larger social issues and concerns. They worked not for the intrinsic rewards of the job or the social utility of their tasks, but because money bought them privacy, the right to tend their suburban gardens while the Great Golfer in the White House governed best by governing least. Golf, being the extraordinarily private game it is, suited them wonderfully well, whatever inner furies it released in them being compensated for by the blessed loneliness of the tramp down the fairways.

Indeed, aside from solitaire, golf is the only game (as opposed to recreations like skiing and sailing) which can be played without a human opponent at all, that abstraction known as par being the perfect substitute for that divot-digging, and otherwise distracting creature, one's fellow man.

Now tennis, though at least theoretically governed by a tradition of polite behavior and honorable conduct as strict (and therefore as pleasing) as golf's, demands not just an opponent, but one with whom you can stand intimate contact for a fairly lengthy period of time. And though, when things are going badly, we spend a good deal of time—far too much, in fact—in self-hatred, the persons or persons across the net from us are essential to us. We must, of course, try to beat them, but we must care for their well-being, too. For we are bound to them by the invisible lines the ball traces back and forth across the net in its endless travels from our rackets to theirs and back again. Their presence, their efforts, break in on our self-absorption, arrest the involuted spiral into melancholia (and impotent, club-breaking rage) that seems to me the golfer's inevitable lot.

"Only connect"—it is one of the most famous phrases in modern literature, the imperative (too long unrecognized) of our age. And tennis is, unlike its rival sport, a way of doing so, a game which presents a perfect balance between inner needs and outer demands. It seems to me

superficial to trace the popularity of the game merely to television's discovery of it, or the rise of open tennis, or the need to discover a game that makes smaller demands on our time and our increasingly limited space than golf does. It seems to me completely natural that as the lonely crowd began to disperse under the impress of large historical forces we would turn to this game which had for so long been waiting for more of us to notice it.

Here, of course, I speak with personal bias. I make my living as a writer, an essentially lonely and self-preoccupied line of work. I don't need or want any more opportunities for introspection. But more and more of us —the majority of the middle-class majority, I suspect—are leading similar lives, lives that drive themselves in upon themselves, which is why more and more of us will turn to this game. It suits our needs just now, suits our needs for intimacy within a structured, reassuringly predictable context, which artfully prohibits our playmates from excesses of intrusion just as it limits the operation of blind chance, which increasingly seems to rule our lives, the very universe we inhabit.

That ancient at Forest Hills—I know the need that forced him out, even on that deplorably crowded day, to his club and his match. Those black men on a distant island—we found a way of sharing a moment in time in a period and, indeed, in a particular place, where it is difficult to find a common ground. The subtle essence of this (to my mind) greatest of games lies in the unique sense of sharing it encourages. One feels it even in the heat of a great tournament, sees it in the flash of a grin, which may come as well from loser or winner, at the conclusion of a well-fought point, in the muttered "yup" of a ranked player as he acknowledges the winner he cannot retrieve. This, one feels, will survive prosperity as it survived neglect. It is finally why we play no matter what inconveniences the world imposes on us, what defects of physique or temperament we carry onto the court. We seek here what we seek everywhere —a moment of grace in a graceless world. And we find more of them here than we do anywhere else. At least I do. For all I know, even Jimmy Connors may be able to say the same.

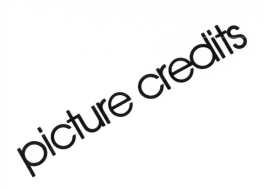
picture credits

Chapter 1
10-11: AS/NL. **13:** MD. **14:** Gary Gladstone.
17: Christopher W. Morrow/Photo Researchers;
Rocky Weldon; MD; MD. **18-19:** All MD except **New Yorker**
cover by Saxon. **21:** MD. **22-23:** John Zimmerman.
24: Ken Regan/Camera 5. **26:** John Zimmerman; Greylock Camp.
27: John Zimmerman. **28:** MD; Peter Borsai.

Chapter 2
30-31: Racquet & Tennis Club.
33: Wadsworth Atheneum, Hartford, Connecticut —
Ella Gallup Sumner and Mary Catlin Sumner Collection.
34: NYPL; NL. **35:** NYPL. **36:** NYPL. **37:** AS/NL; NYPL.
38-39: AS/Racquet & Tennis Club. **41:** NYPL.
42: The Forbes Magazine Collection, New York. **44-45:**
The Staten Island Historical Society.
46: PF; The Bettmann Archive. **48:** NYPL.
49: AS/NL. **50-51:** NYPL. **52:** BB.

Chapter 3
54-55: UU. **57:** BB. **58:** UU. **60:** BB. **61:** PF. **62-70:** UU.
72-73: UU; BB; PF. **74-75:** UU. **76:** PF; UU.

Chapter 4
78-79: AS/NL. **81:** PF. **82-83-84:** UU. **85:** PF.
86-87: Private Collection/Photograph courtesy Kraushaar Gallery.
88-89: UU. **90:** David Namias/Naomi Rothschild Collection.
93: BB. **94-95:** BB; PF; UU; UU. **97:** UU.
98-99: AS/NL; Metropolitan Museum of Art, bequest of
Miss Adelaide Milton de Groot.
100: BB; UU; UU; UU. **102-103:** PF; Keystone Press Agency;
PF. **104:** UPI. **105:** PF.

Chapter 5
106-107: MD. **109-112:** PF. **115:** MD.

116-117: WW. **118-119:** MD. **120:** PF. **121:** PP.
123: MD. **124-125:** PF. **126:** PF; PF; Keystone Press Agency.
128: BB; UU. **129:** UU. **130:** UU; WW.
131: UU; UU; Fred Kaplan.

Chapter 6
132-133: PP. **135:** WW. **136:** WW; PP; WW; WW; WW.
139: WW; UPI. **140:** PP. **142:** BC. **143:** Horst Schäfer.
144-145: PP. **146-147:** Fred Kaplan.
148: PP. **149:** Horst Schäfer. **150:** BC.

Chapter 7
152-157: PP. **158-159:** UPI. **160:** PP. **163:** MD.
164: WW; BC. **165:** PP; PP. **166:** MD. **168:** BC.

Chapter 8
170-171: Ken Regan/Camera 5. **173:** UU.
174-175: Naomi Rothschild Collection. **176:** UU. **177:** BB.
178-179: Aberdeen Art Gallery & Museum, Scotland.
180: BB; WW. **181:** UU. **182:** Naomi Rothschild Collection.
183: UU. **184-185:** UU. **186:** BB; UU; UU. **187:** UU.
188: UU; others PF. **190:** PP. **191:** Ken Regan/Camera 5.
195: PP. **196:** BC. **197:** Al Satterwhite/Camera 5. **198:** MD.
199: Ken Regan/Camera 5; Al Satterwhite/Camera 5. **200:** PP.

Chapter 9
202-203: BC. **205-210:** BC. **213:** MD. **214:** MD; BC.
215: BC. **217:** BC. **218:** Kevin Fitzgerald.
219: MD; BC; BC; MD. **220-223:** MD. **224-225:** BC.
226: Kevin Fitzgerald. **227:** Kevin Fitzgerald; BC. **229:** BC.
230: MD. **231-237:** BC.

Chapter 10
238-239: MD. **241:** Paul G. Schutzer/PF.
242: MD. **243:** BC. **244:** BC.